This is Not a Leaders

Part leadership book, part business book and 100% true, this is like hearing a wise, honest, and humorous mentor finally tell you about the world of business as it is and how to find your place in it.

Many leadership books are either shallow (focusing on only one element of leadership), narrow (examining leadership out of context), or biased (selling an idealised model). This book seeks simplicity without being simplistic and focuses on the reader in their context rather than describing other people's leadership in theirs. It sets out 20 rules for success that draw on Emmanuel Gobillot's 20 years of experience advising high-performing leaders. Each rule is presented in an engaging, instantly recognisable true story that helps current and aspiring leaders to look differently at their own situation.

Best described as a leadership development programme, this book takes you on a fast-paced, three-step journey from *what* it takes to be a leader, to *why* you can be one, via *how* to succeed.

Described as 'the first leadership guru for the digital generation' and 'the freshest voice in leadership today', Emmanuel Gobillot is one of the world's foremost thinkers and authorities on leadership. Author of six UK and US bestselling books, and ranked among Europe's most sought-after speakers, Emmanuel consults with CEOs and executives globally. A French national, he moved to the UK in 1985.

This is Not a Leadership Book

20 Rules for Success

Emmanuel Gobillot

Routledge
Taylor & Francis Group

NEW YORK AND LONDON

Designed cover image: Jelena Mirkovic

First published 2024
by Routledge
605 Third Avenue, New York, NY 10158

and by Routledge
4 Park Square, Milton Park, Abingdon, Oxon, OX14 4RN

Routledge is an imprint of the Taylor & Francis Group, an informa business

Library of Congress Cataloging-in-Publication Data
Names: Gobillot, Emmanuel, author.
Title: This is not a leadership book : 20 rules for success / Emmanuel Gobillot.
Description: New York, NY : Routledge, 2024. |
Includes bibliographical references and index. |
Identifiers: LCCN 2023041577 (print) | LCCN 2023041578 (ebook) |
ISBN 9781032639376 (hardback) | ISBN 9781032639369 (paperback) |
ISBN 9781032639390 (ebook)
Subjects: LCSH: Leadership. | Leadership–Case studies. |
Organizational change. | Success in business.
Classification: LCC HM1261 .G6328 2024 (print) | LCC HM1261 (ebook) |
DDC 303.3/4–dc23/eng/20231127
LC record available at https://lccn.loc.gov/2023041577
LC ebook record available at https://lccn.loc.gov/2023041578

ISBN: 9781032639376 (hbk)
ISBN: 9781032639369 (pbk)
ISBN: 9781032639390 (ebk)

DOI: 10.4324/9781032639390

Typeset in Sabon
by Newgen Publishing UK

To the thousands of executives I have met,
the hundreds of clients I have been privileged to
work with,
the tens of managers who mentored and shaped me,
and the one person who stood by me through it all.

Contents

Acknowledgements

You don't have to spend very long working in an organisation to realise that John F. Kennedy was right when he claimed: 'Success has many fathers, but failure is an orphan.' The publishing world turned this upside down by attributing the success of many to one person alone. These acknowledgements are my chance to put right the fact that the cover carries only my name.

In the following pages I will share stories of tens of people and lessons inspired by hundreds. They are too numerous to name which is why I dedicated this book to them. There is however one person I want to give special thanks to. Shaun O'Callaghan and I met in a maternity hospital over twenty years ago as our respective daughters were about to be born. The friendship that ensued turned into a lifelong conversation about organisations. I have been lucky to collaborate with him on a number of assignments and learn from him on every one of them. This book would be an article had it not been for his insights.

The fact that you are holding these pages at all, however, is down to a team of people who believed it was worth investing their time, their effort and even their money in them.

I first met Matthew Smith when I published my third book. He was my editor then. His encyclopaedic knowledge of the publishing world helped shape my career, his wise counsel, my writing. He became my publisher when he established his own imprint and latterly my agent through his literary agency Exprimez. He was the one who advised me to partner with Routledge/Taylor & Francis for this book. It was a decision that was easy to make and one I have not regretted.

The team at Routledge has been a delight to work with. Under the direction of Senior Editor Meredith Norwich, whose project this was, and with the guidance of Assistant Editor, Bethany Nelson, and Production Editor, Stacey Carter, my clumsy ideas became lessons and chapters. Special thanks also go to copy editor, Ingalo Thomson, for going beyond correcting my words and grammar to give my sentences structure and rhythm. Their work is proof that while we live in a world where we can publish anything, anywhere, at any time, it doesn't always mean we should. Great publishers make bad books good and good books great. I'll let you be the judge of how far they took this one.

Talking of you, it is also you I want to acknowledge. There would be no books without readers. I have been lucky that many of you have shown enough interest in my previous books for me to be given license to have another go. For this I want to thank you.

To reassure JFK, I want to make it clear that whilst all of you and the people named above are the parents of my success, I, alone, bear responsibility for any mistakes left in the following pages.

Introduction – The world does not need another leadership book

Leadership books won't make you successful. You don't have to believe me. Just look at the evidence.

Great leadership is tightly correlated with high employee engagement yet, year after year, employees in every sector, every industry, everywhere around the globe are reporting abysmal levels of engagement. The rise in leadership books, articles, podcasts, training courses, and development programmes hasn't dented the great wall of leadership mediocrity we are crashing against.

While I wouldn't argue that there is a strong causality between the rise in leadership literature and the lack of great leadership, I can't fail to notice the poor at best, inverse at worst, correlation between the two. Leadership books are being published but great leaders are not being made. The reason is simple.

Leadership books are either shallow, narrow, biased, or, worst of all, all three!

They are shallow because they focus on one element of leadership to the detriment of the interactions this may have with others.

Most cover a single idea that would fit into an article and then enhance this with examples and tips, such that the single idea can be turned into a book. That one idea can be incredibly valuable. You cannot be a great leader without emotional intelligence, for example. But the value of a single idea is also limited. Emotional intelligence will only make you successful if you have all the other skills and attributes great leaders need. You need more than one book for insights into these.

The problem with shallow, one-idea books, is that reading two might not help either. They often contradict each other. What are you to do if you read 'The Authoritative Leader: Commanding Your Way to Success' followed by 'The Collaborative Leader: Empowering Teams for Lasting Results'? One emphasises command and control while the other promotes collaboration and empowerment: which is the right one to read and follow

DOI: 10.4324/9781032639390-1

for success? And given both are probably right, how do you know when to do what?

With shallow books, your success will depend on correctly assessing your needs (unlikely if you are like most human beings) as well as having an inordinate amount of time (also unlikely) to read an inordinate number of books to fulfil these needs.

Because they are shallow, leadership books focus on aspects of leadership without ever linking them to the whole. You can only succeed if you understand what leaders are for. Shallow books don't allow for that.

Leadership books are narrow because they examine leadership in isolation from its context.

When I was pitching my first book, the first publisher I met asked me to describe what kind of book I was writing. I said I was working on a book about leadership and organisation effectiveness. He stopped me in my tracks and said, 'Before you go any further you need to understand that in bookstores there is a leadership shelf and an organisation effectiveness shelf. Choose your shelf.'

While today bookstores tend to have fewer shelves for business books, online booksellers have even more segmented sections. There are over 20 subcategories to choose from on Amazon in the business management and leadership category. It's no longer about choosing a shelf but choosing an exact placement on one. Yet success depends on applying the right leadership skills, at the right time, in the right context. That's at least three shelves!

Going on a leadership programme that isn't tailored to your environment is always suboptimal, yet leadership books are designed this way. They may help you with the skills element, but when it comes to applying such skills at the right time and in the appropriate context, you're on your own. You'll have to do the work, assuming you have the time and inclination to do so with no guarantee of success.

I see this often with the tomes written by academics. They are evidence based, thoroughly researched, often tested, and usually well written. They are deep but narrow. They focus on one aspect (be it psychological, contextual, structural ...) of leadership and unpack this. They may well be 'must reads' but there are many of them and you need them all to get the full picture.

Without aggregation, in isolation, narrow books are more likely to confuse than to help. Academics understand that leadership is inherently complex, but the practitioner needs simple solutions. In their aim to make sense of the complex, academics forget the context.

You can only succeed if you know how you must act in your time and context. Narrow books don't cater for that.

But perhaps, worst of all, leadership books won't contribute to your success because they are biased.

Take the following 2023 findings from McKinsey and Company, the consultancy familiar to senior leaders globally (not least because quite a few of them used to work there). In an article entitled 'New leadership for a new era of thriving organizations', the authors argue that leaders need to make five critical shifts: from profit to impact, competition to cocreation, command to collaboration, control to evolution, and expectation to wholeness.

I am not about to disagree with the findings; I argued for pretty much the same shifts in my book *Leadershift* published about 15 years ago. I am neither making the point that I am more far-sighted than these authors (arguably I was biased sooner), nor that in 15 years nothing has changed. I simply want to point out that these shifts have not and still do not represent the reality experienced by much of the working population today. What I was doing when I wrote *Leadershift*, and what the McKinsey article does now, was to describe leadership not as it is, but as it could be or ought to be.

Leadership writings from consultants do this all the time. They may not directly try to sell you a product or a service, but they do want to sell you an idea. Biased books are designed to sell you an approach, a set of behaviours, or a model representing an ideal leader. They may well be researched and may well be right, but they represent an aspirational state. Biased books are about an ideal rather than a real view of leadership today.

There are other biases at play in leadership literature. Books written by, or about, actual leaders are also likely to derail you on your road to success. Their experience is real, their stories first hand, but their methodology and intent are biased. They are biased by both hindsight and attribution.

They are the equivalent of lending your reading glasses to someone. It would be incredibly lucky if borrowing them would help them see perfectly. The number of environmental variables that would need to align for someone else's experience to fit your context is so huge that their advice will at best be unhelpful and at worst make you a poor copy of someone else.

You can only succeed if you know why you want to lead today. Biased books don't care about that.

So, if shallow, narrow, and biased books don't allow for, cater for, or care about what you need to succeed, you can see why we don't need another leadership book.

I am sure you are familiar with the Belgian surrealist painter René Magritte's picture called 'The Treachery of Images'. It shows an image of a pipe with 'ceci n'est pas une pipe' (this is not a pipe) written underneath. Consider this book the 'Treachery of Books'. It may look like a leadership book, but it is not a leadership book.

Consider this a book about leading rather than leadership.

It is not a book that aims to be simplistic about leadership. It is a book that seeks simplicity in its practice. It is not a book about other people's leadership. It is about you leading in your context. More importantly, it is not a book about leadership as it should or ought to be. It is about leading as it is.

This is a book about what leaders are for, how they become great, and why, with dedication and the right focus, you too can succeed.

It is based on real examples from over 20 years of helping build, develop, and grow leaders and organisations. I have consulted around the world, in private and public sector organisations. I have met thousands of executives and worked closely with hundreds.

To avoid any chance of this book being shallow, narrow, or biased, I have applied several strategies. I have analysed the notes I took throughout my career. I have read the business books you probably won't have time to read and the academic papers you probably shouldn't take the time to read. I have identified the variables (be they behavioural, environmental, or skills-based) that contributed to success. I have investigated the relationship between them and determined the minimum number of variables with the maximum impact.

I ended up with the 20 rules in this book. I have illustrated each of them using a personal professional story. I have removed the names of the people or companies involved to enable me to tell the stories as they happened, thus removing the need for editing out elements and thereby creating bias.

The rules are organised into three parts titled What, How, and Why because they cover broadly three themes: What it takes to be a successful leader (i.e., the ground rules), How to become a successful leader (i.e., the actions), and, finally, Why you want to be a successful leader (i.e., the motivation). They are discussed in that order. The book does not need to be read sequentially, although, given that some chapters contain cross-references to rules other than those covered in the chapter in question, it is probably better to do so.

Finally, to enable you to choose the rules that you may want to focus on most, I have finished each chapter with a short summary.

I have worked to make the book readable, informative, and effective but, above all, true.

Part 1

What

'What did you want to be when you were little?' is not as frequently asked as 'What do you want to do when you grow up?'. Its relative rarity however does not make it any less legitimate a question. In fact, the answer to 'What did you want to be when you were little?' is far more revealing of a person than asking a child about their dream.

I have witnessed countless 'fireside chats'. You know, the session in a workshop when a senior leader enters a room and sits down amongst eager employees to tell them about her leadership journey. You must have been to a few in your time. If you haven't, don't worry too much; I'm sure you will. Who knows, someday it might even be you, sitting there, recounting your life story.

What has always struck me in these sessions is how lives explained backwards always seem to make sense. Invariably the story always follows what novelists and script writers call a perfect narrative arc.

It will start with the exposition. The leader will disclose something about her upbringing to introduce you to her world. She will follow this with an incident, a key moment in her life where something goes wrong or is unintended. This moment will embolden her towards some action. Tension will rise to a crisis point. This is where we get to the climax. The excitement of the story. The part where she realises that not all is lost, and that if she can conquer her fears, she will conquer the world. The denouement and resolution will come in a neat package that explains why she is here today, able to share the wisdom she gained through a life well lived.

It is tidy. It is engaging. It is powerful. It is also a lie.

The philosopher Søren Kierkegaard famously said that 'Life can only be understood backwards, but it must be lived forwards'. Who am I to disagree. The problem is that these fireside chats are not about lives understood. They are about lives rationalised. They seldom contain the lucky breaks, the inaction, the 'going with the flow', the 'I did it because I couldn't

DOI: 10.4324/9781032639390-2

do anything else', the 'it was the only thing available', the doubts and the 'I have no ideas'.

Listening to them makes you think executives are living the dream. You can almost hear the narrator of the film, speaking in that deep voice with the obligatory American accent, saying 'From the age of five, she always dreamt of becoming a Chief Financial Officer. Life had other plans, but she wasn't going to let that get in her way.' That's why the question 'what did you want to be when you were little?' is such a valuable one. Sure, gifted raconteurs will be able to go from 'a vet' to 'a CFO' in a few chapters, but the story will have to take some unexpected turns.

So, what did you want to be when you were little? Chances are you either wanted to be a noun or an adjective.

The noun would have been an occupation. More than likely, it was a vocation. You wanted to be a vet, a teacher, a doctor, a singer, or an ambulance driver. Few children ever want to be accountants, or leadership development professionals for that matter. I wanted to be a petrol pump attendant if you must know.

The adjective would have been an outcome. You might have wanted to be famous, happy, rich, or just plain old successful. Whatever your answer was, it would have been as much a reflection of the culture you grew up in as a reflection of your inner desires.

The same is true for the success narratives that leaders share at fireside chats. Their stories reflect the culture they inhabit as well as conveying the one they are trying to create. It is not so much their story they tell, but rather a story of what they believe leaders should be. Their success is not so much explained in order to reflect as it is rationalised in order to influence. They are more focused on the 'why' of their stories (i.e., why am I telling you this) rather than the 'what' (i.e., what happened).

But, just like children, if we are to be successful, we need to reconnect to what we want to become. Defining this will help us decide if we are the product of cultural forces (i.e., we feel we ought to be it) or truly charting our path (i.e., we want to be it). Just like children, we need to differentiate between the nouns and the adjectives. While the nouns inform the position, it is the adjectives that will give us motivation.

The first part of this book contains the rules that will help you define your 'what'. We will look at what success means, what leadership is, what value you bring and what values you have. This section is designed to help you answer the two questions that matter on your way to success: Do you know what you are setting yourself up for, and do you have what it takes to achieve it?

Rule 1

You can succeed

Vancouver, Canada

There are three questions I am always asked. It doesn't matter if I am speaking at a conference, facilitating a meeting, running a workshop, or just having a conversation: at some stage I will be asked one of them, a combination of any of them, or all three.

The first is 'how do you pronounce your name?'. Few understand the innate characteristic of the French language that is to add silent letters to words. If you just ignore the 'ls' (they are only there to transform the 'i' into 'iy' for some reason) and the 't' (we have no idea why it's there), you get something like 'go-be-yo' and that's about right!

The second is 'are leaders born or made?'. I always answer it with care as I am aware that it is asked in search of hope. Either the person asking the question thinks they have been born with the enormous burden of command, or they are hoping that the hours of hard work and devotion spent in mastering the elusive skill will eventually pay off.

The third is 'what makes a great leader?', which is always, without fail, asked with a plea, in the eyes of the questioner, for a short and simple answer, preferably arranged in a list of no more than three bullet points.

Given that I was speaking in Canada that day, the host spared me the first question, thus raising one in my own head: 'why can't all countries be bilingual?' However, I couldn't escape the other two. The audience member asking had been clever, though. He managed to fit both into one sentence: 'What in your view makes a great leader and are these attributes gained through nature or nurture?'

I might have come over as flippant above, in my description of the questions, so, let me be clear, these are important questions. They are also perfectly legitimate questions. After all, if there is such a thing as a leadership gene, then leadership development becomes suboptimal for those without it. If, on the other hand, leadership is developed, then we had better be sure that the characteristics we are trying to develop do indeed lead to success.

DOI: 10.4324/9781032639390-3

There is, however, a reason I was surprised on this occasion, which is why, despite having been asked the question countless times in my career, this particular instance has stuck in my mind for so long. On that day, on that stage, the answer was staring the questioner in the face. Literally.

The organiser had asked me to be on a panel to take questions from the audience. To my delight (given how rare this was then and continues to be now) the panel was the most diverse I had ever seen. I was the only white middle-aged man on stage. We were so diverse we looked like a stock photo straight out of an organisation's annual report or a diversity PowerPoint deck. The only thing we had in common was that we were all successful experts and leaders in our fields. Not that any of us probably thought of ourselves as such, but these were the terms the moderator had chosen to use in introducing us.

Up to that point, my stock answer to the question 'are leaders born or made?' had always been that having been present at the birth of my two children and spoken to quite a few parents, leadership is not the first word that comes to mind when describing a newborn (although their subsequent ability to get you up at night may be a sign of some kind of leadership characteristic).

My somewhat longer response was that even if, one day, we do identify a leadership gene, we will also see that many carriers never become leaders. A leadership gene will not, in and of itself, guarantee success in the same way as an excess in testosterone does not necessarily make you a marathon runner. Leadership is the ultimate equal opportunity employer. Some may find it comes more naturally, some may find it takes a lot of work, but all should remember that success is never guaranteed but always possible.

On that day, in that room, the answer to 'is there a predisposition to and a recipe for success?' was, however, on the stage. The panel's presence was proof positive that becoming a successful leader is open to anyone. Hence the name of our rule and the fact that it comes first – you can succeed.

Now I grant you that this line is unlikely to feature on a motivational poster. For this to happen I should have written 'you will succeed'. 'You will succeed' carries a guarantee that readers like and publishers can sell.

But I don't know you. I don't know if you'll put in the work or follow the rules. I don't know where you are going and where you are on your journey. I don't know anything about your context and the people you work with (as we will see later, your success depends on other people too). So, a guarantee of success may sound appealing, but it is also deceitful.

I have no idea if you will succeed. I do know, however, remembering the people on that Vancouver stage, that there is nothing holding you back.

I do know that there is nothing that can stop you. I do know you can succeed.

'You can succeed' comes first becomes it points out that success is down to you. Sure, some people are more privileged than others. In fact, way back in 2007 when I wrote my first book, 'The Connected Leader', I mentioned research by the international network of business leaders, the Caux Round Table, that shows how privileged I am, and, given that you are holding this book, you are too.

It stated that if your home has something other than a dirt floor, you are in the top half of the world's population. If your home has a roof, a door, windows and more than one room, you are in the top 20 %. If you have refrigeration in your home, you are in the top 5 %. And if you have a car, a computer, and a microwave, then you are in the top 1%.

I am therefore well aware that some people will have had a better start in life than others and better support throughout it too. But even then, only they, themselves, can be architects (if not always builders) of their own success. Whatever your situation and whatever privileges you may or may not have, the fact remains that you can succeed.

There are two steps you can take to turn 'you can' into 'you will'. First, define and refine success. Second, become lucky!

Let's look at defining and refining success first. I know it seems obvious but while I have met many people who said they wanted to be successful, few can tell me what that means. And for every person who can articulate the 'what' of success there are at least ten unable to tell me why they want to succeed. Yet, knowing what success looks like for you, as well as why you want it, is critical to achieving it.

The 'what' gives us a marker. The 'why' gives us a reason and some options. Without either, you are unlikely ever to succeed.

Let's take an example. Let's assume you want to succeed in your career. It is a noble aim. It is not, however, detailed enough. What does 'succeed in your career' look like? Would you articulate it in terms of a role that you aspire to be promoted to? What about if that role was to disappear? Where would that leave you?

We can frame it better. You might want to say 'I want to have reached the highest echelon of the hierarchy in the bank I work in by the age of 50' or 'I want to be promoted to the role of partner in my firm by the time I reach 30'. Management trainers would be happy with us being able to state SMART goals (Specific, Measurable, Achievable, Relevant and Time-bound). But we are still missing a part. We are missing the 'why'. We know what you want to get but we don't know why you want it.

Imagine you achieve either goal. You are the CEO of the bank at 48 or promoted to partner aged 25. In the process, however, you never managed to make any friends. You got the position, but you are tired and lonely. Are you successful then? These are neither rhetorical nor judgemental questions. Maybe you would still feel successful. That's fine by me. It is your life. The point is that, to formulate an answer, you have had to go beyond defining success in terms of 'what' and have had to start thinking about 'why' these promotions mattered to you beyond other aspects of your life.

Success is an emotional state that is difficult to quantify and being reductive in its definition will reduce your ability to achieve it. That is why you need to expand and refine your thinking. You need to think about specific elements of success. The more specific you are in identifying these elements, the more opportunities you will have to achieve them.

What is driving you to want to be the CEO? Maybe you want to be recognised as an expert in your field. Perhaps you want to command respect and have an impact on the lives of others. You may seek financial security and independence. It could be that you crave being listened to and in demand. You have a what, a why and some elements.

Now think about a woman in her 30s. People are eager to see her perform on stage. Audiences look up at her in awe. She has a strong voice that delivers powerful messages. She commands not only attention and respect on the part of her followers but also drives them to action. She is more financially successful that most of us will ever be. She is at the top of her game and has graced the cover of magazines. She is without a doubt a success. She has achieved all the elements we set out above.

This last paragraph could as easily be about singer Lady Gaga, famous for all the right reasons, as it could the disgraced founder of Theranos, Elizabeth Holmes, famous for all the wrong reasons. The point is that there are numerous ways to achieve the same success goals. There are different ways to lead.

Understanding the 'what' and 'why' of success helps you define your options. Refining them into core elements helps you expand them. It gives you flexibility and having flexibility is critical to seizing opportunities. This is where our second step comes in – become lucky.

Luck plays a huge part in success. Yet, if it is acknowledged at all, it is often described in dismissive terms. The quote 'I'm a great believer in luck, and I find that the harder I work the more I have of it', wrongly attributed to Thomas Jefferson, is a common feature of motivational speeches. It underlines how reluctant we are to acknowledge the place hazard plays in our life (I guess us consultants and authors can't really make money out of serendipity). Making your own luck is not, by definition, something you can do. Yet, while you can't make your own luck, you can take your own luck.

We have already seen above how accidents of birth can define a trajectory, if not entirely dictate its outcomes. That is not to say, however, that you don't have an impact on how many opportunities come your way and whether you seize them. To become lucky requires two habits – curiosity and saying yes.

Curiosity is key to identifying luck. If you only define the 'what' of success and seek out to achieve it, you are likely to be so focused on the goal that you become blind to the road. You don't spot the opportunities around you. You no longer question the road you are on. By remaining curious and looking around you will see opportunities to achieve elements of your definition of success beyond the obvious.

Which gets us to 'saying yes'. Being lucky requires taking chances. Luck is just an opportunity that has been seized. The more opportunities you say yes to, the more you will multiply your chances of being lucky.

The reason that defining success in terms of components is so important is that it makes it easier to say yes. If, for example, you are offered a project and all you think about is your trajectory towards a 'what' goal (e.g., 'does it get me closer to that CEO position'), you will judge the opportunity differently from how you would assess it when doing so through the lens of components of success. It may be the project is a sideways move rather than an upwards one, but it may get you some of the success components you crave sooner than if you waited for the promotion opportunity.

The default should always be 'saying yes' to any and every opportunity that comes your way unless there is a complete absence of success elements in what they offer.

This was my answer to the audience member standing in front of us that day in Vancouver.

'Look in front of you. We are all different and yet we have all been introduced as successful leaders in our fields. The only thing that differentiates us from you is that we got asked to be on the panel and said yes to the opportunity. We got the call because there is something others see in us that drove them to call. But what they see is merely the result of work and application in our field rather than some inherent characteristic. The reason we apply ourselves to this work is because we have a clear sense of what success means to us in terms of the elements of our lives and have found these compelling enough to keep us on the road to success, being able to identify opportunities and remaining open to seizing them. We said yes because it meant something to us to be here. This is not a mix of biology or determination but rather a mix of clarity and working to be lucky.'

It's a long and clunky answer but it has the advantage of being true! Yet, while it might say something about success, it does not tell us about success in leading which is what our next rule is about.

From rule to lesson

Rule 1 – You can succeed

Throughout the book I will summarise every rule into its core lessons. So, what does our first rule have to teach us?

You can only be successful if you are clear about what success is for you and why you want it. Be careful not to be distracted by end goals in terms of destination (e.g., the trappings of success like position, money, etc.). Focus instead on why you want these things and what elements they will bring to your life (e.g., the ability to impact others so you feel you make a positive difference to your community).

Having defined both what you want, and why you want it, you need to set out to maximise your ability to achieve it. This means being curious about what is going on beyond your natural and immediate environment (i.e., your organisation, sector, professional network) so you can see opportunities that are not obvious. You also need to ensure you say yes to any and every opportunity that comes your way when such opportunities offer you even the slightest chance of fulfilling any of the elements of success you seek.

Rule 2

Line up your screws

San Francisco, USA

My first publisher categorised books in terms of flight routes. She'd talk about a 'long haul' to describe a book you would have to read in more than one sitting as you would on a plane when interrupted by a couple of meals. She would muse about a 'London to New York'; a book that would take roughly seven hours to read. She would talk about the commercial success of 'London to Amsterdam' short motivational story books.

But that day, overlooking the clouds, I hadn't even managed to write enough to fill the 15-minute underground journey from my apartment to my office. I was flying high over the ocean but risked crashing in my publisher's esteem. I have never been good at working on planes. For me, flights mean too many distractions, too many people, too much anticipation, and always some nervousness.

Sometimes the nervousness is about whatever I will be doing at the other end (I have never stopped being nervous about any engagement). Sometimes it is about the flight itself (I have never been a 'good flyer'). Today it was about both.

I was on one of the bumpiest flights I had been on in a while, on my way to San Francisco, to address an audience at Google's headquarters. It was my first time visiting the famed Googleplex. Four years after its IPO, two years after it entered both the Standard & Poor's 500 index as a stock and the *English Oxford Dictionary* as a verb, despite the global financial crisis and its ensuing recession, Google was part of the zeitgeist. It was the first of my clients my kids had heard of and were interested in. I was worried about the flight, worried about my speech, and worried about the jetlag. I wasn't in the best frame of mind when I landed at 5 p.m.. But that was about to change.

On the cab from the airport, I had planned for the evening. Check in, have dinner, try to stay awake long enough to get a full night's sleep before my speech the following day. Part one of the plan went well. Check in was fast. It was when I arrived in my room, however, that part two suffered a

DOI: 10.4324/9781032639390-4

delay. As I went to switch on the light, I couldn't help but become fascinated by the switch. I know! It's not something that normally happens to me either.

This light switch had three buttons, a gauge that looked like a thermostat, and eight screws: four on top of the switches and four underneath. Again, this was nothing to get fascinated about. But I was becoming so interested that I decided to call Reception to ask if I could have access to more rooms (unoccupied of course) just so I could look at their light switches.

This being San Francisco, the young man at the front desk didn't seem fazed. He made my request sound perfectly acceptable and routine. So, off we went. We did four floors and seven rooms before I concluded what, by now, on my part at least, had become a fully fledged research project. What I didn't know then was that, more than a decade later, I would still be discussing the light switch in my room. My picture has been seen by audiences across functions, industries, and the globe. You see, this light switch was the most compelling picture of leadership I had seen in a while.

I know some people might assume that I saw in this switch an analogy for leadership. Such thinking might run something along the lines of 'leadership is about shedding light onto issues' or 'it's all about clarity'. Others may see the thermostat as prescient when defining leadership as 'creating a climate for excellence'. But my reasoning was nothing of the sort.

It was the screws and more particularly the screw slots that had made me stop. Each screw had a single slot and each slot was aligned to the next, thus creating a perfect horizontal line across the four screws at the top and another one below. There are several reasons why an electrician fitting a light switch might want to ensure that screws are aligned with each other.

Maybe, like me, and I grant you this is weird, they take an aesthetic pleasure in the alignment. More importantly, though, there are also safety reasons why they may want to do this. I have been told that in hospitals, electricians are often contracted to ensure the slots on screws are always vertical. This is to minimise dust settling in the cracks. But, more likely in this instance, electricians are told to align the screws so that it's possible to check quickly for wire movements inside the plug (i.e., if the screws become misaligned, something has moved).

Finding out the correct explanation was simply a matter of research. It could be that the screws automatically aligned: that in some way when the screws were tightened, the slot automatically fell in the horizontal position. That was unlikely, but research is research. You can't assume.

If all screws were aligned, in all the rooms, then all electricians or an electrician (although I doubted the entire hotel had been wired by one person) had been told to align the slots.

However, if all screws, in all rooms, were not universally aligned, something else was going on.

In the other two rooms I could visit on my floor, all the slots were aligned. Everywhere else in the hotel, though, none were. So, the alignment wasn't automatic. There was a particular electrician going around San Francisco who lined up her screws. That electrician gave me my second rule of leadership success – line up your screws. Here's how.

Call it a leftover from my French education, but I believe it is critical to define anything clearly before you embark upon discussing it and, in the case of leadership, developing it. With Rule 1 we looked at what success means for you and what it would give you. Logically, given this is a book about leadership success, we need to define leadership. So, what has a successful, screw-aligning, electrician got to do with the definition of leadership?

At work, unlike in other areas of life, it is leaders, not followers, who appoint leaders. So, the first thing about successful leadership at work is to ensure you are followed. It seems obvious. If you turn around and no one is behind you, you are not leading anyone. But having followers is not enough. You need them to do something. You need their effort. There are two kinds of effort you need.

The first is contractual effort. As the name implies, this is about doing what you are contracted to do. Contractual effort is easy to get. It is easy to get a human being to do something. Anything. All you need is a big enough stick or carrot. You can be nice about your demands. Some leaders have become masters in the art of lovely coercion. Regardless of the strategy you use, the desired outcome is the same – do what I tell you to do.

The problem with contractual effort is that when you say to people 'do what I tell you to do', they do just that. They do exactly and solely what you have asked them to. They do so, even when they know that what you are asking them to do is daft. They do so, even if they know you will fail because of their actions. They do so, even when they know something better could be done. They do so because you want it so.

The other type of effort is what is known as discretionary effort. The concept is the same as discretionary spend. Discretionary effort is the amount of effort you have left after you have tackled everything you are contracted to do.

I am sure that at some stage in your working life you have found yourself fully engaged. You were lost in time. You would have done whatever needed to be done to achieve excellence, regardless of whether it was in your contract or not. That's discretionary effort.

Leaders require both types of effort on the part of their followers.

There is value in contractual effort. Without it, you would have enormous organisational costs. You would have to redefine roles every time you needed something done. The contractual costs, which organisations are designed to minimise, would go through the roof. Contractual effort is also critical when faced with a crisis where delays might cost dearly.

The issue is not about relying on contractual effort, but about relying solely on it. If contractual effort is all you have, you are not leading. You are constantly pushing and pulling. Contractual effort doesn't need leadership. It only requires an adept HR department.

There are two problems with the very notion of contractual effort which you can't get around unless you add discretionary effort. The first is that you must know absolutely everything you want. If you can't articulate exactly what you want, nothing gets done. Given how changeable the present has become and how uncertain the future is, this is unlikely ever to be the case.

The second problem is that you will have to make every decision because, given that you are in charge, people will only do what you tell them to do (not anyone else). Taken together, these two issues dramatically slow down your ability both to anticipate and to respond to change.

This can only be mitigated through discretionary effort. Countless studies, over decades, have demonstrated its financial benefits which far outweigh its very minimal cost. It is unsurprising. There is value to people doing what they know to be right rather than just what is demanded.

There is value when people do what needs to be done rather than just what has been asked of them. There is value when people articulate solutions to problems you haven't seen yet rather than just solving the ones you have identified. There is value in people letting you know you are making a mistake rather than rejoicing when you have made it.

My San Francisco electrician displayed both types of effort. She turned up for work, wired the switch, and the lights turned on. That's contractual effort. Then she lined up the screws. Thus, she made it easier for future colleagues to see if a switch might have developed an issue and for weird French guests to delight in the beauty of horizontal screw slots. That's discretionary effort.

Our electrician was not only doing her job. She cared enough about her job to go beyond what she was contracted to do. This could as easily have been about picking up the trash behind her than it was lining up her screws. She knew that excellence is not some kind of abstract strategy but is about simple, small acts that make a huge difference.

Sure, you may not have noticed the aligned slots, but you would have noticed the electrician. You know she is more than likely to take her shoes off when she enters your property. You can be pretty sure that while she is working on your switches, if she spots something wrong with the light fittings, she will make sure to tell you. If it's a simple fix she may even do it for no extra charge. You know she'll care. She won't just do what she is contracted to do well but will go over and above to ensure you are delighted. If she is self-employed, she'll succeed. If she works for a firm, it'll succeed.

Think about it this way. If you need any work done in your own home, don't you want the electrician who will align the screws?

Leading is not about coaxing/coercing people to get stuff done. Leading is about creating the conditions for others to positively engage with a goal. This means creating the conditions for people to want to release their discretionary effort.

We will look again at this in Part 2 of this book, when we discuss the 'how' of success. The reason we have Rule 2, however, is because, amid everyday work, when under so much pressure to do so much, it is too easy to default back to contractual effort. Carrying Rule 2 in your head will ensure you don't lose sight of this. Remember a few paragraphs ago when I told you about your own experience of discretionary effort? The difference between the fully engaged you and the disengaged you was down to one thing. It was about leadership. Your boss had either remembered or forgotten the rule about always ensuring that the screws line up.

The role of leaders is about creating the conditions for engagement. They can only create these conditions if they are clear about their value and how this is perceived by others. Let's turn to this with our next rule.

From rule to lesson

Rule 2 – Line up your screws

Wanting effort from our followers is not enough. We need the right kind of effort. It is easy to get people to do anything, but we want them to do the right things right. This requires them not only to do what they are contracted to do (contractual effort) but to do this positively (discretionary effort).

Because of their reliance on the leader being right and always being there, tactics that are pushing, prodding, coaxing, and coercing will always, eventually, derail success.

Leadership is about creating the conditions for people to engage positively with a goal. Only this marriage of contractual and discretionary effort guarantees short-, medium-, and long-term success. Leadership is about aligning the screws.

Rule 3

EST and ER do not spell value

London, England

The cameras, the microphones, and the journalists weren't my idea. I admit, though, I wish they had been.

It was a member of the client's staff who had suggested we got professionals involved. 'It'll make it more real,' she'd said. Real was an understatement. Frightening was what it was for many of the participants. But frightening in a good way!

We had designed the workshop to bring together some of the most senior leaders from a global telecommunications company. The objective of our workshop was simple – organise some stimulating input to help the participants map out their business priorities and articulate the cultural choices necessary to deliver them.

We decided to start our four days together with a simple question. It was a legitimate, rather than rhetorical, question, and one that was being asked in the company's retail outlets around the globe: 'why should I choose you?'

That's why the journalists were there. They stood outside our venue like a pack of wolves. As soon as our participants got off the bus from the airport, they pounced. The effect was amazing. Our executives, some media-trained to within an inch of their lives and others media-savvy enough to cope, didn't flinch. They got on with it.

Native English speakers found it easier. Marketing executives had more polished answers. Commercial people almost had their contracts out before the journalist had a chance to say cut. It was fun. It was light-hearted. It was a great way to start the day. Above all, though, it helped me develop a new rule.

The rule emerged as the workshop team and I sat down in the evening to review the journalists' footage, identify key messages and themes, and prepare the feedback we planned to give the following day. It was about 10 minutes in that we realised we all had a smile on our faces.

DOI: 10.4324/9781032639390-5

We weren't enjoying the video with pride in our eyes and the sense of a job well done, in the way a parent might when watching a school play. We were enjoying it more in the way you and I might enjoy the guilty pleasure of watching a mindless TV series. Watching our executives speak was like watching a bad reality TV show. It was like an episode of *The Apprentice* or a spin-off of some first-date show.

All the words being used ended with ESTs and ERs. We are the fastest, biggest, leanest, simplest, cheaper, better, nicer, and easier. It was all me, me, me! If this had been a speed dating session, no one would have got a call back. Even if they had, the relationship would be unlikely to last. You may be able to develop a contractual relationship if you are the richest, fastest, leanest, but what happens when your competitors catch up? What happens to the relationship when you become poor, slow, and overweight unless it is based on something other than ERs and ESTs?

The only way our executives could articulate the value of their product was either in relation to attributes of their business or by homing in on the product itself or in contrast to their competitors. It was all about them. I am sure that they thought that, by implication, whatever they talked about was good for the customer, but they never felt the need to make the leap. As a result, it was the kind of date where you'd arrange for a friend to call halfway through so you could put a stop to the endless 'aren't I great' conversation!

But why does it matter? Our executives weren't dating or trying to get a job on *The Apprentice*. It matters because, whether you are trying to secure the discretionary spend of customers or the discretionary effort of followers, you must be clear about the value you bring and articulate this in a way that resonates. Contractual spend and effort may well cope with ESTs and ERs, but they won't get you discretionary anything.

Of course, understanding your strengths is important but they alone won't give you a rounded picture of your self-worth. It is only when coupled with an understanding of your weaknesses and areas for growth that you will get a clear sense of who you are as a leader.

Before you start worrying that I have some kind of fixation on dating, the reason it matters is that leadership, just like so much else in business, is fundamentally about relationships. And there are two sides to relationships (the leader and her followers) which means you cannot know your value unless you know what others see as valuable. If you want a relationship you must care about the other party and talk with them as much as you care about talking about yourself.

Determining your value is therefore about understanding both your unique attributes as well as the unique needs of your potential followers (as opposed to simply comparing your own attributes to those of others).

Only then will you be able to create a strong enough magnetic pull for them to want to follow. When it comes to understanding our value, we need to look beyond the classic list of personal achievements and competitive comparisons.

I have always been frustrated by leaders' lack of understanding of their worth. While we will discuss the potential sources and remedies for this in Rules 7 and 8, in the main it comes down to our reluctance to be open with others about what we value in them. This is true of all cultures, even if some are worse in this regard than others.

Whatever you think of yourself, there are people, in your workplace today, who look at you, thinking 'I wish I was more like them' or 'I so wish I could do what they just did'. They will never tell you and you will never ask them. But they exist. This absence of feedback is an obstacle to understanding your worth. Don't get me wrong. I am not one of these people who advocate a focus on strengths at all costs. I am all too aware of the potential of weaknesses to derail a career. I am, however, clear that you cannot begin to be effective at providing value without understanding what is unique about you.

The first step to establishing your value is to unearth what about you is unique. Doing so will require some work. By all means, do take time to reflect on your skills, strengths, and qualities. Concentrate on identifying areas where you feel you excel but also where others seek your expertise or assistance, as this makes these areas objectively valuable. But don't stop there, or you'll end up like my executives in London and simply find a lot of ESTs and ERs. Instead consider what unique attributes and experiences brought you these particular ESTs and ERs.

Then seek feedback from others. Start with people you trust to be open, and with whom you know you will be safe sharing your own doubts. Ask them for their honest opinion on what they appreciate or find valuable about you. Don't be tempted to ask about what you could do better or improve. I know you want to better yourself and I'm sure we all can. But this is not the point of the exercise.

Armed with these findings, consider your impact on others. Leading is an exchange of energy (i.e., creating the conditions for the positive engagement of others as seen in our last rule). In this context, your unique attribute can only become your unique value if it impacts others. You need to be able to recognise the contributions you make and the difference you can create for others. Identify times at which you have positively influenced others' lives, whether personal or professional. Recognise the contributions you make and the difference you can create.

Mix these reflections with observations. Pay attention to how others respond to you in various situations. Notice if they seek your advice, input, or support. Consider when others rely on you for certain tasks.

How often do they do it? Why? These interactions are the best indicators of the value you bring to others even if others are not always aware of it or able to articulate it clearly.

In the same way, identify instances where you positively impact the well-being and happiness of those around you. Discretionary effort-driven followership is an emotional act, not always an intentional, rational one. Emotions play a part in value. So, consider the emotional support you provide, the positive influence you have on others' mindset or motivation, and the ways in which you contribute to creating a positive environment.

Finding out what is unique about you carries a couple of risks.

The first is that you, mostly inadvertently, become a caricature of yourself. It is all too common that once people have been given a label, they become that label. I am sure I am not the only one to have seen people take feedback from numerous so-called psychometric instruments and play up the label they have been given. Equally, I'm certain many have witnessed the proliferation of introverts or people suffering from imposter syndrome since the popularisation of these terms.

I once asked my UK-based agent for feedback on why clients decided to book me rather than any other leadership speaker. His answer was, 'You're French and you're funny which is kind of a rare combination!' I can't deny the first and think the second is flattering, but what does that tell me?

Well, it tells me that, in my field, expertise does not differentiate. It is taken as a given. It is baseline. The style of delivery is what is important. Being French is an asset only in so far as it means that culturally I approach things differently from, let's say, a more Anglo-Saxon school of thought. Being funny means that the audience is more likely to pay attention and remember. Whatever sense we make of it, though, it doesn't mean I need to turn up to my next speaking engagement wearing a beret and a stripy shirt with a full comic routine prepared.

The second risk is that you become self-centred. You fail to realise that, in the context of your leadership value, what makes you unique or differentiates you is only valuable if it matters to others. 'Funny' and 'French' may not end in EST or ER but they are no more a differentiator to a serious Francophobe than better and fastest are to people who seek dependable value.

This is why, as well as understanding our unique value, we need to understand what counts as value to the people we are looking to engage. What is unique about and shared amongst that group?

Start by clearly identifying the group of people you are trying to appeal to. You can be as broad or as narrow as you need to be. But you need some idea to enable you to target your research. You will then need to work out what brings coherence to this group (be that social, cultural, or professional). What is their purpose and what are their values, beliefs, goals, activities? What is their demographic and cultural make up?

What are the filters through which they will assess your worth? What unique perspectives, principles, or philosophies does the group embody? Looking at the group's internal dynamics (e.g., leadership structure, decision-making processes, and social interactions) will help you.

Determine if there are any distinct features that contribute to the group's uniqueness. You can look at external perspectives, evaluating stereotypes, reputations, or associations attributed to the group. Assess how these perceptions contribute to the group's uniqueness. To help you narrow your findings, look for patterns, recurring themes, or key characteristics that consistently differentiate the group from others. Find what holds this group together. These shared and unique characteristics define value.

Let's get back to our executives. What could they have said differently when looking at their value? They worked for a telecoms company. We know already that they have the largest and fastest network with the simplest and fairest tariffs. At least that's what they told us. The first step should be for them to make sure that their assessment of their value is the same as their customers' reality. But let's assume they are right.

What of the customers in the retail stores they were trying to attract? What is unique about them?

As is the case with telecoms, the segments are rather broad: everyone wants a phone. Our executives belonged to a large global organisation. It wasn't a niche provider, focused on a particular segment (e.g., affluent customers, large corporates, small businesses, etc.). They had products to cater for them all. What does such a large and varied group have in common? My guess, and it is only a guess as I am neither a telecommunication nor a marketing expert, is that they all want to be able to make calls whenever they need to make calls.

So, how could the executives have answered the journalists chasing them as they disembarked a bus on a cold London morning? How about something like 'we care about the calls you make to people you care about' to highlight their dedication to connectivity, or 'you'll never need to call us' to underscore their reliability and simplicity. Again, I am not a marketing professional, so I am sure there are better ways to say any of these things. But the key point here is the shift of focus from 'I' as a leader or 'we' as an organisation to a much more powerful 'you' as customers and 'us' as partners.

After watching the raw footage, we edited it and played a short version in the morning. We discussed it and I'd love to say we came up with something clever I have never forgotten but we obviously didn't as I can't quite remember what we agreed on. We did agree on the rule, though, that EST and ER cannot possibly spell value whether in business or for us as leaders. This is the very reason why our next rule is critical.

From rule to lesson

Rule 3 – EST and ER do not spell value

Knowing your personal value helps you define your vision and purpose as a leader. It provides a foundation for creating the conditions necessary to inspire and motivate others to release their discretionary effort.

Your personal value has a significant impact on those you lead. However, as we have already seen, as much as leadership is about you as a leader it cannot exist without followers. This is why defining your value solely in terms of your personal achievements and/or how they compare to others (i.e., with words ending in EST or ER) is fundamentally flawed.

The only way to establish value is to understand what is demonstrably unique and true about you and establish how this helps meet the unique and shared goals of the people you are looking to inspire. Articulating your value helps you engage others and ensure they can act independently from you in order to achieve the objectives you set.

Rule 4

Leading is a moral act

Amsterdam, Netherlands

Only in the Netherlands!

For someone born in France who has lived close to 40 years in the UK, there is something incredibly refreshing about Dutch culture. In France, what you think, and feel, is only deemed of value if it is expressed in more words than are necessary for a clear understanding. In England, what you think, and feel, is better left unsaid. But in the Netherlands, you say what you think regardless of how it makes others feel.

You say it clearly. You say it plainly. If you think it and feel it, you say it. It doesn't really matter what the impact of what you say is. Whoever you say it to won't be shy about telling you what they think either. It's straightforward, easy, and unfiltered. It's bizarre. It's weird. It's rude. But, it's refreshing!

That day, I had been invited to an event in Amsterdam. The organisers had asked me to speak for about an hour, take questions from the audience, and stay behind to sign copies of my newly published book. It was my first book. It was the beginning of my writing and speaking career. I was nervous and excited but, above all, I was grateful. That's until I was asked the dreaded question.

I mentioned in our first rule 'you can succeed' that I am always asked three questions – 'how do you pronounce your name?', 'are leaders born or made?', and 'what makes a great leader?', but that's not quite true. There is a fourth question that comes up in most Q&A sessions. It can take different forms. Some might ask 'who is the leader who best demonstrates the type of leadership you advocate?', others more simply 'who is the leader you admire the most?'. Whatever form it takes, though, it is a question I dread.

I dread it because I know that there is no way I can answer it in a way that will satisfy the person asking it. They don't want me just to name anyone. They want me to name someone they have heard of. They want

DOI: 10.4324/9781032639390-6

a Nelson Mandela, an Indira Gandhi, a Steve Jobs, a Sheryl Sandberg, or whoever happens to be famous and part of the zeitgeist in that culture, at that time. The problem is that I don't know any of these people.

I have met famous people. I have met some of the rock stars of business, sports, and politics, as well as, on occasion, stars of rock and roll. Usually this happens at conferences, as they exit the stage and I enter it or vice versa. All I know is what they say and what their handshakes feel like. I have met them, but I don't know them.

I have also read many biographies of so-called great leaders. I know what they or other people have written about them, but I don't have any first-hand experience of how they work. Whether I have met them or read about them, all I know is the persona. I do not know the person. How can I, therefore, in all honesty, have a coherent and correct view of their ability to lead? How can I possibly hold as an example or a model someone I only know as a caricature?

There are, of course, many leaders I admire. These are the leaders I have had the privilege to work with or observe in my research. But what value is there in me naming them if you've never heard of them?

I never shy away from answering questions in a way that might displease an audience if I know the answer is right, but I never like giving a non-answer. And when it comes to naming the leader I admire the most, I know my answer will come up short.

I also dread the intent behind the question. Is it being asked to judge whether what I have to say is worthy of being heard, some kind of test? Or is it being asked with a view to identifying a role model who can be copied? If it is the former, then I will fail. If it is the latter, then it is my questioner who will.

The good news was that, this time, I couldn't possibly be judged for not having met the person. The bad news was that, despite never having met the person, there was no way I could not have an opinion. I could not give a non-answer.

For that day, on a sunny afternoon in Amsterdam, in a beautiful venue overlooking the canals, I was simply asked 'was Adolf Hitler a great leader?'. Only in the Netherlands, indeed!

This was the first time I was asked that question, but it wasn't to be the last. I would soon find out that conference Q&A sessions are like social media conversations. If you wait long enough, someone will mention Hitler. As a result, I have become all too aware of the dangers of discussing leadership with respect to the second world war and its main actors, or indeed any wars or historical figures.

Only a few years ago the tabloid press, here in the UK, headlined on a leadership consultant who had showed pictures of Hitler during a government-funded workshop. It is not something I would have done.

Indeed, I make it a personal rule never to discuss the second world war and its actors or use military analogies in my work. I am breaking that personal rule, here, only to bring out a critical one for success. That critical rule is that leading is a moral act.

Let's get back to the question. Deciding whether Hitler was a great leader or not requires a proper examination of the word 'great' as well as a thorough introspection of our intent in asking the question.

Let's start with the definition of 'great'. I stated in our second rule 'line up your screws' that 'leadership is about creating the conditions for the positive engagement of others with a goal'. I made the point that leadership was about our ability to gain discretionary as well as contractual effort from our followers. In this way, I defined leadership as a skill, and skills are fundamentally amoral. It would be silly to describe the skill of cabinet making, say, as being moral or immoral.

But what about shooting guns? While no one would argue that the inclusion of target shooting at the Olympic games is immoral, even the most ardent defenders of the US second amendment are unlikely to describe the use of guns in school mass shootings as moral. To judge greatness, we cannot possibly disassociate the skill from its application.

Being able to get an entire country to not only follow (contractual effort) but, in many cases, embrace (discretionary effort) murderous and heinous policy cannot be called great leadership. Even if we are ever driven to use the word 'great' simply to indicate the extent to which the skill is displayed, the moral imperative associated with the outcome is impossible to ignore. Leadership as a skill may well be immoral, but leading is a moral act.

This is why I mention the need for thorough introspection of our intent in asking the question 'was Hitler a great leader?'. The fact that he comes up at all is to make a point. It is a kind of leadership 'gotcha' question. The abhorrence of his actions leaves no room for compromise. How could anyone see Hitler as anything other than a monster? It would be morally reprehensible to recognise him as a great leader; that much is obvious. It would be an endorsement of the unconscionable. It would be immoral.

But what if we didn't go to the extreme, and looked at other historical leaders? How about Napoleon Bonaparte? Napoleon restored order from the chaos that ensued in the wake of the French revolution. He left behind a legacy of beneficial reforms, not least of which is the Napoleonic Code, that continues to influence France to this day. France declared 2021 'Year of the Emperor' to commemorate the bicentenary of his death. Surely this is the mark of a great leader!

But can we brush aside the millions of deaths he caused by keeping Europe in a constant state of war for the best part of 15 years? It was

Charles de Gaulle, war hero, leader of the provisional French government (1944–6) and President of France (1959–69), who wrote, 'Napoleon
left France crushed, invaded, drained of blood and courage, smaller than
when he had taken control of her destinies ...' Hardly a picture of great
leadership.

How about another second world war leader? Was Winston Churchill a
great leader? Britons seem to think so. They voted him the greatest Briton
in a 2002 BBC poll. That must qualify him as a great leader.

Brits may wish to celebrate the considerable achievements of Churchill
the war leader. Indians on the other hand may prefer to stress his well-
documented prejudiced views of Hindu social and cultural practices as
well as policies that contributed to the 1943 Bengali famine. The fact that
his statues have become the focal point of so-called 'culture wars' over
recent years point to a more nuanced picture than the word 'great' might
suggest.

The search for great leaders blinds us to the reality of leadership. There
is no such thing as a great leader because there is no such thing as a great
human being. We are all flawed to a lesser or greater extent. But there
is one critical point that emerges from the futile search for the great
leader – while leadership as a skill is amoral, leading as a practice cannot
be. Leading, as an act, is either moral or immoral. We may never have the
impact on society that the leaders I have cited have had. But that is not
the same as saying that our leadership impact is not great. Leading, as an
intentional act, cannot be disassociated from morality.

Rule 1 asked us to define success and Rule 2 defined leading as creating
the conditions for others to positively engage with a goal. Rule 3 forced us
to understand our value to others and express it in a way that resonates
with them. We can do all these things without morality. Yet, as much as
your value to others creates success, it is a lack of values that will make
you fail. The first three rules help us answer the fundamental question
chosen by Rob Goffee and Gareth R. Jones as the title of their book, 'Why
should anyone be led by you?'; however, it is another question that will
determine how successful you can be: 'What do you want to lead for?'

We can define success as personal enrichment and create a legion of
followers who will help us fulfil our aim by using populist ideas. We can
defraud and lie. Many have and many will. Being successful in the short
term does not require morality, but sustaining success does. Nineteenth-
century American minister Theodore Parker said it best when he declared
that 'the arc of the moral universe is long, but it tends towards justice'.

Morality goes beyond legal compliance. It is a set of principles, values,
and ethical standards that guide the behaviour, decision-making processes,
and overall conduct of leaders. It focuses on the impact of decisions on

stakeholders, employees, customers, and society at large. All these things are necessary for sustainable success.

Moral leaders inspire others to do their best, foster loyalty, and build strong interpersonal relationships, resulting in enhanced productivity and organisational success. They possess the courage to make tough choices and are willing to take responsibility for their actions.

Organisations led by morally upright individuals enjoy long-term success. By prioritising integrity, leaders build credibility and trust with stakeholders and the wider community. A leader's moral compass guides them in navigating obstacles with wisdom, fairness, and transparency.

Consider the impact you want to have as a leader. Reflect on the causes, issues, or goals that ignite your passion and the areas where you can contribute the most value. What is the overarching goal you want to achieve? How do you envisage making a difference in the lives of others or in your organisation?

Your purpose should align with your values and passions, giving you a sense of direction and meaning. Leadership may be a skill but leading is a lifelong journey of growth and learning. Your purpose and indeed some of your values will have to change and adjust to remain relevant and stay aligned with your evolving self. You will, over time, shape and refine your understanding of what you stand for as a leader. But stand for something you must.

We have looked at both who you are and what you stand for, but there is a final question that must be asked. Are who you are and what you stand for good enough?

From rule to lesson

Rule 4 – Leading is a moral act

We have defined success. We have defined leadership as the skill of creating the conditions for the positive engagement of others with a goal. We have defined your value and articulated it in a way that engages others. We have outlined the conditions for success. What we haven't yet looked at are the conditions for failure.

Mastering the skill of leadership is necessary to succeed but it is not sufficient. The potential for failure lies not in the lack of leadership skills but in the act of leading itself. Failure will not come from your lack of value, but from your lack of values.

When we want to become a great leader, we tend to focus on two things – skills and followers. We work to master the skills that make us a magnet for others to follow. We work on answering the question 'why should anyone be led by me?'. This may work in the short term, but our shortcomings and eventual failure will become apparent if we have failed to answer another fundamental question which needs to come first: 'What do I want to lead for?'

This is not a skills question but a values question. While the 'why' question enables us to trace a path, only the 'what' question can help us navigate it.

Rule 5

Authenticity is overrated

Kuala Lumpur, Malaysia

Don't believe those who tell you that international travel is all about glamour. I've stayed in some horrible places in my time.

I've been in hotels where the rooms hadn't been serviced for a long time, if ever. I've stayed in rooms that were too hot and rooms too cold, in positions too noisy or freakily remote. I've stayed in rooms so modern that I couldn't work out how to switch on the light, and in rooms so old that they didn't have any. Once, I was woken very early one morning, in Australia, by a call from reception to inform me that the strange noises against my door were the result of an inebriated airline pilot being sick against it (my flight later that day was a particularly nervous one). But this was a step beyond.

I had arrived in Kuala Lumpur the evening before. The fourteen-hour flight hadn't made my night an easy one. I was speaking at an event that afternoon. I wasn't expecting an early wake-up call so the knock on my door at five in the morning came as a surprise. I got up and opened the door. No one was there. I looked down to see if something had been left in front of the door. Nothing was there. I went back to bed.

The resort was lovely. My room was a villa in the middle of impeccable grounds. Check-in had been seamless and smooth with a much-appreciated cold towel and a refreshing fruit cocktail. The service had been great, so I put the knock down to a mistake and tried to get back to sleep.

Five minutes later someone knocked again. I opened the door. I saw nothing. I wondered. I went back to bed. It took me four more knocks and four back-and-forth trips to the door to get annoyed. I blame the jetlag. I normally get annoyed quicker. I called reception for an explanation. 'That would be the monkeys, Sir' was not an answer I had ever received before.

It was the first time that something so annoying put me in such a good mood. I was in a hotel, having a practical joke played on me by a bunch of monkeys living on my roof. That's one of the reasons I remember this

DOI: 10.4324/9781032639390-7

trip. The other is because this is where I formulated Rule 5. Authenticity is overrated.

My speech went well. The event was the annual retreat of a company with presence across Asia. I opened with the monkey story. It drew laughs from some and empathetic nods from those delegates who had been staying at the same venue. I spoke for an hour and then had dinner with the group. I went back to my room hoping for a better night's sleep but looking forward to my early morning call.

Unusually I didn't have to fly out straightaway. I had a few days before my flight back. The CEO invited me to have lunch with him the following day. Halfway through the meal he asked for my help. He explained that a member of his senior leadership team had had a fast upward trajectory and a very successful career driven mainly by his technical brilliance. While he was a respected member of the team, he was now being held back by his inability to connect with and impact the people around him.

He wasn't a bully, a feared or disliked leader. He was just unable to command the respect of his peers and employees in the way that would make him a prime candidate for the executive team. The CEO had tried to help. Feedback had been sought and courses offered. But nothing seemed to have made a big difference. They had discussed engaging the help of an executive coach but, so far, the leader had refused. Until, that is, the day before.

Having heard me speak, he had thought, 'I think he could help me'; or rather, as the CEO put it, 'he thought you weren't like a weird psychologist type, and you might be able to teach him something.' I am not sure what that says about me or psychologists, but I guess that was nice feedback!

The problem is that I am too impatient and too opinionated to be a good coach.

I understand the need for coaching and am in awe of great coaches. I once witnessed a colleague adding an enormous amount of value simply through her masterful use of questions. She managed to take an executive on a journey through his own mind to a place where he found his own answers. Helping him do so, rather than telling him what to do, dramatically increased the likelihood of a successful implementation of his ideas.

Great coaches know what they don't know and understand what they can't understand. Solutions depend on content and context while implementation requires experience and expertise. For these reasons, helping someone think through something can be much more fruitful than advising them on a course of action. I therefore don't have any issues with coaching; I just know I can't do it well.

This may be because, when seeking help, I have been asked 'what do you think you should do', with the emphasis on 'you', by too many bosses who have gone on too many coaching courses. I have also never been able to work out a business model for coaching that would work for me. When you charge for value, it is hard to make a living when you don't think you are adding much of it. The fact that I prefer to work face to face when the work is one on one, and this leader lived on the side of the world, didn't help much either.

I do like to help clients, especially those who have been so generous in their hospitality, but on this occasion I didn't think I was the right person. I told the CEO that the best I could offer was a conversation with his colleague. I would see what I could do and if, as I suspected, the answer was not much, I would, at least, be able to advise on a course of action or recommend a colleague who could provide more help than me. A meeting was set up for later that day.

The meeting was a delight. The leader in question was a fascinating man. He was clearly passionate about his chosen field of expertise. He spoke fast. He had the kind of manic energy that passionate experts have. He wanted to contribute to the growth of the organisation and clearly cared about his team. But, as he saw it, they just weren't getting it.

They saw him as caring more about the outcome than about them, when all he cared about was to make sure they succeeded. They told him he was unable to listen, when all he tried to do was to give them answers to the problems they faced. They felt he was incapable of praise, when he thought their pay was their reward and he fought hard to make sure they were all paid well.

He was puzzled rather than annoyed and thought I would understand because I had mentioned in my speech that authenticity was key to leadership. 'I heard what you said and that resonated with me, because quite frankly I am just being myself. I am being authentic.' He was right, of course. I had said that authenticity matters.

It matters because, by staying true to their values and beliefs, authentic leaders are seen as credible. By aligning their thoughts to their words, and their words to their actions, they show their integrity and inspire trust. Their genuine passion and enthusiasm help them to connect with others at a deeper, emotional level rather than solely a transactional one. Their reliance on their core values to make decisions ensures they don't fall prey to fads and external pressures. The fact that authentic leaders are driven by their internal values and beliefs rather than a need for external validation, means they are much more resilient. If leading is a moral act, it must follow that authenticity is key.

So yes, authenticity matters but, as our leader was proving, it is also overrated. Too often 'I am being myself, I am authentic' is worn as a badge of honour by the inexperienced and ineffective. For leadership success, being yourself is not the be all and end all. Being the most skilful version of yourself is.

Leadership is all about relationships. As such, leadership is all about you but also not about you at all. It is all about you in so far as others want to align with you, but not about you at all because it is the others who must make the decision to align. Claiming authenticity makes it just about you. Practising skilful authenticity is what makes leaders successful.

The idea of skilful authenticity wasn't landing with my interlocutor, though. His view was that either you are authentic or you are not. Trying to make authenticity skilful led, by definition, to inauthenticity. In a sense, he was right: authenticity is generally considered to be a trait rather than a skill.

It refers to being true to oneself, genuine, and sincere in thoughts, actions, and interactions with others. Authenticity involves being honest about one's values, beliefs, and emotions, and expressing them without pretence or artifice. But it doesn't mean that you cannot cultivate authenticity the way you can develop a skill. There is a certain skill in being able to consistently express and embody authenticity in various aspects of life. With self-awareness and self-reflection, authenticity can be cultivated.

I was not then, and am not now, proposing being untrue to yourself to conform to external expectations or social norms. Authenticity is deeply rooted in personal values and integrity. It goes beyond mere performance or learned behaviours. What I am however advocating is that to be true to yourself as a leader means that your impact must be in line with your intent. If it isn't, you are not being authentic, you are simply failing to lead.

Let's take my interlocutor as an example. He wanted his people to succeed. They didn't see it. He wanted to help them by providing solutions to their problems. They didn't see it. He wanted to make sure they got properly rewarded. They didn't see it. These people didn't want him to change his deeply held, and in this case highly appropriate, values and beliefs. His behaviour just did not convey any of them. He thought 'they don't get it'. In truth they simply didn't get *him*.

Just like this leader, at some stage you will feel as though you are being asked to be something you are not. Before you feel that your authenticity is being compromised, just ask yourself two questions: Can I be what they ask me to be? Do I want to be what they ask me to be?

These questions will help you determine if you are facing a skill, will, or values issue. If you can be what they want you to be, then ask yourself why you are not. If it is a skill issue, it is possible to remedy the situation. It won't be easy, but it is possible (and indeed the next section of this book should help you). If it is an issue of will, you should question whether or not the benefit of the change is seen as being large enough to justify the cost of changing. If not, then you need to reframe the problem to make the prize big enough or the cost smaller. If you can't do this, then you may be faced with a values issue.

It takes hard work to change deeply held values, but values can be changed. In fact, most of us will change our values. That's called growing up or growing old. You will need a lot of will. You should go back to working out the costs and benefits. If you do not want to be what you are being asked to be, then you have a case for deciding to find somewhere, rather than something, else to be.

In my experience, when people claim their authenticity is being compromised, it is generally because of flawed thinking. Either they are using this as an excuse because they do not have the will to change or the will to develop the skills necessary. Or they are dismissing others' intent, assuming that they do not share their desire to succeed, their standards, or whatever else they value. Or they are simply blind to their impact.

In most cases it is your ability to lead that will be questioned rather than your ability to be yourself. In fact, too many leaders fear being themselves. They would rather ape what they believe to be great leadership than truly run the risk of being a more skilful version of themselves. They would rather be inauthentic than work with their own authenticity.

In Kuala Lumpur I didn't need to coach, I just needed to help this leader understand what being an authentic leader truly meant. In this case it meant being even more authentic and more skilful. He needed to not only behave in line with his values but be much more vocal about them. He needed to state his intent rather than just follow his instinct.

By being genuine and transparent, he would begin to foster open communication and encourage feedback. If people understood that he was trying to fulfil every one of their needs, they would tell him he was going about it the wrong way. If he actively listened to his team members' ideas and concerns, he would become a skilful version of himself.

That doesn't mean he didn't need to find a coach. To become a more skilful version of himself he would need to understand why he was finding it hard to comprehend what other people valued and see this as legitimate. He would need to work on developing the skills and behaviours that would authentically connect with others. That is the kind of work that great coaches can help you do. They can help you see that authenticity with no care or understanding for impact can quickly become narcissism.

The meeting ended with this leader setting out to find himself a local coach. Meanwhile I just returned to my hotel room to become again the laughing stock for a bunch of monkeys.

Now that we have discussed what you want to do and be, and concluded this chapter by emphasising the need to be yourself with skill, it is time to turn to the rules that govern the 'how' of success.

From rule to lesson

Rule 5 – Authenticity is overrated

'I was just being myself' is a poor excuse. While being true to yourself is necessary to ensure your followers know that you mean what you say, you can only succeed if you become the most skilful version possible of yourself.

Authenticity is key in leadership. By staying true to their values, beliefs, and principles, authentic leaders are seen as trustworthy and credible. When leaders are authentic, people feel more comfortable placing their trust in them, which is crucial for building strong relationships and releasing discretionary effort.

Yet, to be authentic is not enough. Being true to yourself is of no value unless your impact is in line with your intent or the needs of your followers. If your impact does not show your values, you have a skill or a will issue. You need to be more authentic by disclosing your intent through more than just your actions.

If being yourself is not what your followers need, you may be the wrong person in the wrong place or maybe you have the wrong team. In my experience the former is more likely than the latter – even though many leaders prefer it the other way round. In any case only if these two are aligned will success follow.

Part 2

How

Imagine we meet on the street. You stop me and ask, 'Could you tell me how to get to the nearest bakery?' It seems like a straightforward enough question. But, if you opened the contents page of this book and looked at Rule 15, you will know that it's not that simple.

Given that I, literally, wrote the rules, I would do well to follow them. This being the case, my only possible answer to 'could you help me get to the bakery?' has to be 'it depends'. But what exactly does it depend on?

It depends on a lot of missing contextual information. It's a bit like saying 'the chicken is ready to eat' where the meaning of the sentence depends entirely on whether I am standing in a farmyard with a bucket of chicken feed or in my kitchen with a carving knife.

In our case, the answer will depend, firstly, on the starting point. It is somewhat easier to give directions to a bakery a few streets away than one in the next town. It will also depend on whether you want to walk, take public transport, or drive. It will depend on whether I know the area we are in better than you and indeed on how familiar you are with the area yourself. Telling you 'Go back down to Finchley Road, cross over as if you were going to Avie and Marta's Tannin and Oak wine bar and it's two doors down from there' will make sense if you know where you are but will be completely useless if you don't.

If I really want to be helpful, I might also point out that my answer will be dependent on what exactly you need a bakery for. We happen to have four in very close proximity to each other. One is great if you need sandwiches but doesn't have the best bread. For that you need to go to another, but its pastries aren't great. Better baked goods can be had at the third, but for birthday cakes and patisseries nothing beats the fourth one.

I am also assuming that what you are after is directional rather than technical information. Maybe you want to know how to drive. Who knows, maybe what you really want to know is how to start your car or how to use the public transportation system.

DOI: 10.4324/9781032639390-8

Faced with so many possibilities, we make a number of assumptions, probably rightly for the sake of all involved. To simplify things, and our lives, social norms suggest that giving turn-by-turn directions to the bakery we deem the closest is best. It might be suboptimal, but it does the job and stops you thinking I am definitely the person to avoid next time you need anything.

The same is true of leadership development. Asked 'how can I lead successfully?', we answer with turn-by-turn directions. Yet, as I already stated in Rule 1, I know nothing about you. I have no contextual information to tell me what you need. I don't know your starting point. I can't possibly tell how familiar you are with the area. Not knowing the purpose of the trip, I have to make a choice of destination. I have no idea if you require directions or technical information.

For the sake of social norms and ease, leadership development professionals and authors will make assumptions and give you directions to their chosen destination. Just as with the bakery directions, their answers are suboptimal but satisfyingly simple. They also ensure you don't end up thinking that they're the person you should definitely avoid next time you need help. Provided that they answer with skill and grace you might even look forward to asking them more questions in the future.

There is however a problem with the 'road direction' analogy. While it may reflect my age, I chose it to highlight how dated our leadership development strategies are. No one today stops strangers to ask for directions. This is not a reflection on our societies having become less convivial but rather on our technologies having become more ubiquitous. Why stop a stranger when you can ask your cell phone?

Our technologies are so advanced that 'Take me to the nearest bakery' is a pretty pedestrian task for any of the digital assistants on offer today. I mentioned my work at Google in our second rule 'Line up your screws'. What I did not mention was my son's reaction when I told him about their invitation for me to speak: 'What I don't understand is that if they want to know what you have to say, why can't they just google it up?'

Asking a stranger for directions may be nice if you want to strike up the beginnings of a friendship, but why get one person's opinion of the nearest bakery when, to get to the best bakery for croissants, you can ask a machine guided by hundreds of satellites and backed up by hundreds of reviews to choose the fastest route there, given current traffic conditions.

We don't yet have a sat nav for success, so we end up having to ask hundreds of strangers, via books, videos, articles, each with different biases, views, and directions. There is, however, a way to build your own leadership GPS to answer the question, 'How do I lead for success?'

This is what this next section is about. In it, I won't give you techniques and tools for success – there are already too many out there; instead, what I will do is give you a leadership positioning system that helps you work out where you are and what to focus on to help you plan your journey to where you want to go. The rules will help you map out the terrain. They will help you understand what drives you and how to capture what drives others. They will show you the unavoidable 'must see' landmarks on the road to success. They will help you ask the right questions and make the right choices to succeed.

Rule 6

Empathy is grossly overrated

Zürich, Switzerland

We were in Switzerland, but we could have been anywhere. The delegates at the event were from all over the world. I was amongst finance professionals, but I could have been speaking with delegates from any industry. We were in 2022, but we could have been in 2002. The conversation we were having was similar to many I have had over the years. It wasn't even the first time someone made a quip quicker than me. It was, however, the first time someone made *my* quip before I did!

As is often the case when discussing employee engagement (the theme of the event I was speaking at), someone came up with the 'Golden Rule'. He said, 'It's not that complicated. You just treat people how you would like to be treated.' This was a notion understood by the entire room. Most countries and religions have a version of the Golden Rule.

I hadn't expected another delegate, quick as a flash, to say, 'You'd better hope your boss isn't a masochist then!' That was my quip. I had been using it for years. Not only did I really think that I'd come up with it, but worse, it never got as many laughs for me as it did for this delegate. I felt cheated! I guess I must not be as original as I hoped in my style of delivery. But I'm not bitter! The proponent of the Golden Rule wasn't offended either. He took the joke as it was intended and laughed. He did however want to clarify what he meant.

'What I mean is that I want to be treated as an individual. I want people to treat me as me and, by the same token, I want to treat them as real people too. I guess what I'm really talking about here is empathy. If we have empathy, we have engagement.'

I had been beaten to my own quip, so I wasn't about to be beaten to my own rule. As he finished his sentence I got my opportunity. 'OK, let's talk about empathy, then, because I have a rule for leaders. Empathy is grossly overrated.' This is our sixth rule.

DOI: 10.4324/9781032639390-9

Of course, I understand the value of the Golden Rule. It makes sense in the context of good social interactions and, in the main, even if it can appear self-centred, the idea of reciprocity is a sound one for relationships. But for leaders, doing unto others as they would like to be done to themselves carries issues. Not least of all is the fact that they are not a representative sample of the human population. They are different by the very nature of their role. If they were like everyone else, they wouldn't have been appointed. The idea of treating people like you when they are nothing like you isn't that good.

I should therefore have been impressed at this delegate's flip from a self-centred interpretation of the golden rule to an other-focused understanding of it via empathy. But empathy bothers me. As much as one should hope one's boss isn't a masochist if following the Golden Rule, one should also be wary of sadists when discussing empathy.

You see, unlike its much older cousin sympathy, empathy is a relatively new concept. At its simplest, sympathy can be defined as sharing the feelings of another while empathy is understanding their feelings without necessarily sharing them. It is therefore possible for someone to be empathic and use their understanding of your feelings to cause pain. By definition, empathy does not guarantee positive engagement.

Countless research papers have been written about the dark side of empathy, and in particular how it can lead us to poor decision making. A study shows how when people were told the story of a little girl in urgent need of life-saving treatment, they invariably saw it as obvious that she should be prioritised for treatment. Who wouldn't. We can all empathise. It never occurred to them that this very prioritisation would deprioritise others, thereby endangering them. It is easier to empathise with, and therefore prioritise, the little girl we know than the little girls we don't.

And if you think the above is more a problem of perspective (i.e., people need to be told about all the other little girls) rather than empathy, you're in for a shock. Studies conducted in conflict situations have shown that empathy is the mechanism through which we become polarised. When we take a side, we take on the emotions of this side. As a result, we become even more entrenched and extreme in our support for that side. It is hard to empathise with the other little girls when we've already backed *our* girl.

This brings us back to the problem with authenticity that we discussed in our last rule. When we mix up 'being myself' with 'feeling like you' we end up with a myopic view of reality and a tribe to reinforce it. We aim our actions at ensuring others feel what we believe they should feel and reject them if they don't feel that way. It's not much of a recipe for engagement.

But even without going to the dark side of empathy, understanding how someone feels does not explain why they feel this way. Say that you intellectually recognize that I am angry. That tells you something about my state of mind but nothing about where that state of mind comes from. I could just as easily be angry with you, the situation we are in, or indeed at something I have just remembered my children did last night. If you don't know what caused a feeling, you can't change it. The understanding brought about by empathy may well be important, but it is in no way sufficient for engagement.

Of course, sympathy, the sharing of feelings, does not really help us as leaders either. While the ability to be emotionally aligned to another person helps us move beyond the potential intellectual detachment of empathy, it is not immune to drawbacks.

Imagine being a leader in a crisis. There's a fire in the building. You see the people around you in distress. What happens next? Well, if you react with sympathy and start feeling deep distress too, the answer is: nothing happens. And nothing is certainly not what your followers are looking for from you. Sympathy enables you to connect emotionally to your followers but it is not enough. On its own, sympathy is of no use for engagement either.

So, given that we are wired for both sympathy and empathy and therefore can't ignore them, how do we deal with them? How do we use them? The answer to these questions lies in understanding what followers look for in their leaders.

The first thing we look for in a leader is 'does she get me?'. Does she understand what it is like to be me? Does she understand my desires? Does she speak my language or, at the very least, understand it? She does not have to be like me, nor does she have to like me, but would she actually spend time with me and I with her?

This is the proverbial 'would I have a beer with that person?' question, much beloved of journalists as they seek to explain the appeal of a particular politician (thus ignoring the view of all non-drinking voters). On that measure it would appear that empathy and indeed sympathy help.

But it is the second part of what we look for in our leaders that neither sympathy nor empathy helps us deliver. We want our leader to do something about how we feel. We go from 'does she get me?' to 'will she help me?'. We don't want her to understand or feel our plight in order to be like us. We want her to want to do something about our plight in order to make us a better version of ourselves. In effect, we want her to channel her empathy and sympathy into positive actions.

This is why my answer to the participant speaking about empathy wasn't just 'empathy is grossly overrated'. That would have been somewhat petulant and aloof. My full answer was more detailed. I explained that when it comes to leadership, instead of discussing empathy, we should be talking about compassion. This may seem like a minor difference, but it is a major one when it comes to engagement.

The problem with compassion in leadership in general, and in business in particular, is that it is seen as, and this is probably the nicest way to put it, 'wishy washy'. It's feels weak and a bit pathetic. We can't help but think that someone who exhibits compassion is looking for self-gratification and those in need of it are too weak to alleviate their own suffering. Compassion is seen as a bit old-fashioned and worthy, or somewhat romantic and poetic. These are not adjectives that sit easily within the business lexicon.

It is this 'deficit-based' view of compassion – pitiful people coming together with those in search of self-satisfaction – that makes it seem weak or wicked. But compassion is actually the secret weapon of engagement and the key to leadership success.

Research, going all the way back to Maslow (of pyramid fame), highlights a number of characteristics that successful leaders share. There are two in particular that drive the level of engagement identified by Maslow when he studied people he described as 'operating with peak experiences' (the likes of Abraham Lincoln, Thomas Jefferson, Albert Einstein, Eleanor Roosevelt, Benedict Spinoza, and Aldous Huxley).

First, these leaders were all what he described as 'reality-centred' rather than 'self-centred'. They could easily distinguish between the reality and their assumptions. Second, they were 'problem-centred' in that they had an insatiable thirst for solutions. Not only do these two elements offer a perfect summary of what I have outlined we look for in our leaders, but they also give us a perfect definition of compassion.

Compassion is active empathy. It is never accepting the status quo but instead challenging the environment in search of solutions to followers' plights (i.e., being reality- and problem-focused). It is compassion that helps leaders secure the engagement of their followers through demonstrating that they share their values.

The point of compassion is that it marries the advantages of empathy (understanding the feeling) with the benefits of sympathy (feeling the predicament others are in) without falling for the pitfalls of manipulation (using the feelings of others for your own ends) or over-attachment (becoming so enmeshed in a situation that you become paralysed by it).

Compassion is about knowing and feeling what others feel but being driven to do something to change these feelings.

This is why this rule is the first of our 'how' section. It enables us to map out the terrain for our leadership positioning system. Compassion helps us understand the reality and seek a destination. Without it, we can't release discretionary effort.

In order to develop compassion leaders can take four steps. The first step is to get familiar with observable reality (i.e., what you are actually seeing). Leaders need to act as anthropologists in their own tribes. They need to genuinely listen (i.e., listen to understand rather than respond) and truly watch (i.e., watch to see rather than simply spot) what is going on around them (we will come back to this in Rule 9 – See and be seen). Without listening we cannot tap into the observable reality we may decide to change. Without watching we may change the wrong thing.

The second step is to check the expression of the behaviour (i.e., if what you think you are seeing is actually what it is). Checking our understanding of how someone feels is not easy. The best way to start is to have data-driven conversations. For example, use phrases like 'when you say ... am I right in thinking you mean ...?'. Better still, explain your feelings in order to understand theirs. Start with 'when you say X that makes me feel Y'. This kind of conversation is hard but the more concrete you make it, the safer it sounds.

The third step of developing compassion is to check the source of the behaviour you see (i.e., where what you see comes from). Of course, checking with someone might be the best option here, but given that often they don't even know why they feel the way they do this tactic does not guarantee success. The best way is to have non-invasive conversations (i.e., conversations that leave the other party free to participate or not). Asking 'are you ok?' is too vague. We always say yes. Be more concrete. 'I can see you look stressed about this; what is bothering you?' Making the feeling concrete changes the tone, and asking an open question emphasises the offer of help rather than demanding an explanation.

The fourth and final step in developing compassion is the action step. This brings us right back to the Golden Rule at the beginning of this chapter. Its advantage is that it is action focused. 'Treat people as you would like to be treated' or 'do unto others ...' both start with active verbs.

If compassion is about action, its definition, too, needs to start with an active verb. Compassion is about treating people the way they want to be treated in order to get them beyond how they feel currently to a place where they feel at their best. Regardless of whether your boss is a sadist or a masochist, that definition will make them effective!

A key question remains, though. How do you make sure followers are motivated to go on the journey with you? This is where our next rule comes in.

From rule to lesson

Rule 6 – Empathy is grossly overrated

Understanding where people are at is key to knowing where you are starting from on your leadership journey. Knowing how to deal with how they feel underlines engagement. This is why so many leaders talk about empathy.

Unlike sympathy (feeling the way others feel), empathy (understanding how others feel) is intellectual. As such it does not mean that you value or validate how they feel. Just as sympathy might lead you to do nothing, given that you could be as stuck in negative feelings as your followers, empathy can lead either to inaction as you don't acknowledge the root problem or to the wrong action as you seek to exploit the way others feel.

The key to engagement is to reframe sympathy and empathy as compassion. Compassion is having an intellectual and emotional understanding of how others feel combined with a willingness to change this for the better. It is only through compassion that leaders can channel the energy of others towards the attainment of a goal. Without compassion, discretionary effort cannot be released.

Rule 7

Only death demotivates

New York, USA

Maybe it's just me, but I am always nervous when I reach passport control at an airport.

I know I haven't broken any laws. I know I haven't lied. I know I am not carrying anything for anyone else. I know my papers are in order. I know all of this, and yet I am always, without fail, a little bit anxious. This, in turn, makes me even more nervous because I worry that agents might interpret my anxiety as guilt. And it's always worse when I arrive in the USA. US airports and border agents are all intimidating.

On this spring day, at JFK airport, however, I was to meet, for the first time (and to this day the last time also), an American border agent with a sense of humour. He had a dry sense of humour, but a sense of humour nevertheless.

I was on my way to a meeting at the United Nations headquarters. As is customary when working with the UN, my contact had issued me with a 'laissez passer' – an official letter meant to facilitate access to less welcoming countries. As I travel on a French passport and was going to the USA, I had assumed I would not need it for entry. I had folded it in my passport and forgotten all about it.

March 2003, however, wasn't an easy month between America and France. The then French Minister of Foreign Affairs, Dominique de Villepin, had given an impassioned speech at the UN against a proposed invasion of Iraq. As a result, France was seen as the leader of a group of countries opposing the American-led coalition. Franco-US relations were far from an 'entente cordiale'.

French fries had been rebranded freedom fries. The makers of French's Mustard had had to issue the statement 'The only thing French about French's Mustard is the name', to avoid millions of American boycotting the brand. This is ironic as, had they boycotted it, Americans would have borne a greater resemblance to French citizens (especially this one born in Dijon) who, for decades, had avoided this most bizarre of condiments!

DOI: 10.4324/9781032639390-10

As I approached his desk, the border agent looked at my French passport with a smirk. The UN letter fell out of it. He duly opened and perused it. With a slight crease at the side of his mouth betraying a hint of a smile he uttered words I would never forget. 'So, let me get this straight. You are French and you are working with the UN. Do you really expect me to let you in today?'

I guess it was my sheepish look that made him laugh. I relaxed and he proceeded to ask the usual questions. The first was 'what kind of business are you in?'. When I replied that I was a leadership development consultant and that my job entailed running workshops and making speeches he seemed rather impressed: 'Oh, you are a motivational speaker.' This was the starting point of my formulating Rule 7 – Only death demotivates.

I've been called a motivational speaker a number of times. I don't dislike it (it's not the worst thing I've been called) but I can't say I particularly like it either. The idea that having me speak to anyone is motivating is strange enough, but the notion that motivation can be outsourced to a speaker is truly baffling. Here is a tip: if you ever find yourself in need of booking a speaker because your people lack motivation, you have a problem no speaker will ever be able to fix. You clearly don't understand human motivation. But then again, who can blame you?

Motivation is one of those complex topics every leader cares about, but few have the time to dig deep into. With over twenty different theories that seek to explain why we do what we do that's hardly their fault. The only difference between them and me is that I have time to look into these things because it's my job to do so. So, while I won't be wasting your time by summarising each theory, I will tell you some of the things they have in common and all of the things you need to know to succeed.

First, all of them, bar none, agree on one thing. We are all motivated. That's right – as one of my old mentors once told me, 'If you ever find yourself declaring someone demotivated, check for a pulse.' That's my biggest problem with being called a motivational speaker: it implies that my audience needs motivating. It never does. Motivation is present in all of us. As our rule states, only death demotivates. We are all driven to do something. Whether this something is what others want us to do is another matter and lies at the root of the 'motivation misunderstanding'.

Leaders assume that their role is to motivate people which is why they are so keen on empathy in order to understand how people feel. The truth, however, is different and, as it happens, much simpler to execute as it does not require us to become psychologists. Our role, as I stated in Rule 2, is *not* to release the discretionary effort of others. It *is* to create the conditions for them to do so. The same applies to motivation.

Our role is not to motivate people. They already are motivated. Our role is to ensure that their motivation is guided towards the achievement of our goal. This is why we need compassion rather than empathy. We need the willingness and wherewithal to create the conditions for people to engage. There's no need to manipulate them; we only need to manipulate the environment. And that's a whole lot easier given that we, as leaders, hold the levers that shape the climate and culture of the workplace.

The second thing all theories agree on is that we have two types of motivation – extrinsic and intrinsic. As the names imply, extrinsic motivation is about doing something because of external factors (e.g. reward and punishment) while intrinsic relies on internal factors (e.g. the doing is the reward). Our behaviour is impacted by both.

We may be tempted to think that intrinsic motivation is more valuable that extrinsic motivation. We may assume that discretionary effort is, by its very definition, the product of intrinsic motivation alone. But we need to remember that behaviour is a complex mix of both. For example, people are at their best when their company has a strong purpose they can align to, but we do well to remember that they'll stop showing up if we stop paying them.

Similarly, we should be careful when pulling the extrinsic motivation lever as it can directly lower intrinsic motivation. It is common for someone who enjoys something to try to turn it into a job only to find out that turning a hobby into a side hustle can quickly become a hassle.

The lesson here is that both intrinsic and extrinsic drivers need to be considered when creating the conditions for the release of discretionary effort. As leaders, we can't ignore either. Pulling extrinsic levers can damage intrinsic motivation. But never pulling them might result in someone never being given the opportunity to discover the intrinsic reward of an activity they would not have engaged in unless extrinsically motivated to do so.

The third and, for our purpose, final area which all theories of motivation agree on is that behaviour is not always a good indicator of motivation. Imagine you see me give a speech. I seem to enjoy it and let's assume you judge me rather good at it. You conclude that I look pretty motivated. The question is by what? The answer is you don't know!

Maybe I am motivated to speak because standing on a stage with people looking up at me makes me feel important. It validates me. Maybe I just get motivated by sharing ideas. I get a sense of self-worth from helping other people grow. Maybe I just enjoy being liked. I get energy from seeing people laugh. Maybe I am motivated by knowing that I will get a fee for my speech which helps me do more of the things I actually enjoy. Or even, maybe, I am not motivated at all but pretty good at faking it.

Arguably, if you have booked me for a speech, or are in the audience, it really doesn't matter what motivates me as long as I give a great speech.

And this is the problem with behaviours not being an indicator of motivation. We only start to question motivation when the behaviour is suboptimal. You don't care about what motivates me until I give a bad speech. Yet, if we only care about what people need when we don't like what we see, we will always be too late in providing it. Creating the right conditions for motivation matters as much in a high-performing climate as it does in a low-performing one.

These three commonalities help us define our role. A leader's role is not to create motivation, but to create the conditions for people to direct their motivation towards a goal (first commonality). To succeed we must understand how extrinsic levers impact intrinsic drivers (second commonality) without assuming that the behaviours we see are an indication of the motivation we seek (third commonality).

If the commonalities between motivational theories help us define our role, how do they help explain how to fulfil it? I promised at the beginning of the chapter to tell you all you need to know to succeed. I can summarise this in three words: choice, community, and competence. If you remember these three Cs and understand how the commonalities impact them, you will succeed in helping people display their motivation at work.

Let's start with choice. We can only be intrinsically motivated if we are given the option to be ourselves. We must have the freedom to choose the way we act. Only when we have autonomy will we display engagement. Trying to control employees through tight objectives, deadlines, and rewards is much more likely to reduce their intrinsic motivation than align it to the goal. When people's choices are curtailed, their motivation is frustrated, and their behaviour becomes suboptimal.

When you declare people demotivated it is more than likely the result of their freedom to act having been curtailed. Creating the conditions for employees to release their motivation means that leaders must define the end (by being both clear about the goal and the required standards to meet this) and let go of the means.

The fact that motivation is best expressed when we have the autonomy to make personal choices does not mean that we only care about ourselves. This is where the idea of community comes in. Human beings are at their most motivated when they are connected to something greater than themselves.

This desire to interact with and be connected to others drives our own sense of self-worth and contributes to our growth. The absence of a supportive environment results in dissatisfaction and destructive behaviours. In practice, these behaviours will either be control behaviours (e.g., power plays and self-aggrandisement) or withdrawal behaviours (e.g., lone-ranger work).

To ensure motivation is released, leaders must maintain a strong sense of community within a group. They should ensure that the extrinsic levers they pull to encourage personal accountability do not damage the sense of belonging to a greater community. In the same way as giving choice demands a clarity of goal, the community variable requires that this goal be placed into the greater context of purpose.

After choice and community, the final element we need to focus on to create a climate favourable to the release of motivation is competence. In a way, competence is the expression of choice and community. It is our desire to develop a level of mastery that enables us to contribute at our best to the environment around us.

Where choice was about having control of the means if not the end, competence is about developing the ability to master those means to reach the end. Where community was about belonging to a nurturing environment, competence is about contributing to it.

Competence is the element we find the easiest to judge. Our bias for measurement makes it easy for us to decide if someone is competent or not. This is why the third commonality of motivational theories (behaviour is a poor marker of motivation) was so important to highlight. It is not because someone lacks competence in terms of outcome that they lack the drive to be competent.

Of course, competence is about ability. As another mentor of mine used to say, 'You can teach a turkey to climb a tree, but it is a lot more cost effective to hire a squirrel.' But the key to competence is to understand that not everyone who can't climb is necessarily a turkey. They may as easily be an uninspired squirrel.

What competence calls for is not feedback – no one in the history of mankind has ever been motivated by the words, 'Can you come to my office? I have some feedback for you.' Competence calls for attention. We want to know that we are being recognised for who we are and understood for what we seek. Our starting point as leaders needs to be that everyone comes to work with the intent to do their best. If their best is not good enough, it is our job to find ways to increase their competence, knowing that they are likely to want this as much as we do.

Taken together, choice, community and competence shape an environment that enables us to line up our screws. These three levers create the conditions for the release of innate motivation by minimising the risks of extrinsic levers diminishing intrinsic drivers. Leaders must shape an environment that is nurturing to individuals in order for them to make the best choices to increase their competence. Our role is not to direct and coax motivation. By giving people our attention and support, we enable motivation to express itself and flourish.

The border agent at JFK airport might have been funny but that does not mean to say he didn't take his job seriously. Arguably, his sense of humour was much more likely to put me at ease, and as a result, answer his question in a less guarded way than I might have done had I something to hide. He was given the choice to behave in the way he wanted and was much more competent as a result. But above all, he didn't seem to feel the need to intimidate in order to create impact. This underscores how, in order to impact the behaviour of others, it is not just their motivation that matters but ours. This is what our next rule is about.

From rule to lesson

Rule 7 – Only death demotivates

Motivation is complex but the key lesson from Rule 7 is that it is not our job to create it.

As leaders we need to recognise that everyone is motivated. Our success lies in our ability to create an environment that leads people to release that intrinsic motivation in the pursuit of our goals.

To do so there are three levers we need to focus on. The first is choice. This is about giving people the autonomy to be themselves in the pursuit of a clearly articulated goal with accepted standards. The second lever is community. This is about creating a sense of purpose that is greater than the individual. The third is the lever of competence. This is about ensuring that people see the opportunity to grow and experience the support to do so.

Rule 8

Power up

Hong Kong, China

It is often the most invisible people who shine the brightest light.

Standing proud on the edge of Victoria Harbour, with views over Hong Kong Island, the Peninsula hotel has been an unmistakable Kowloon landmark since its opening in 1928. Its grand colonial façade, housing a majestic door guarded by two giant stone Foo Dogs, is magnificent. The hotel's legendary fleet of green Rolls Royces lined up in front is impressive. Hong Kong aficionados might argue over which hotel has the best location, but none doubt that the Peninsula service is unrivalled.

I was in Hong Kong to facilitate a workshop for a client's senior leadership team. The Peninsula was to be our base for three days. The company was doing well! Early in the morning, I walked around the meeting room to make sure everything was in place. Over the years, these walk-arounds have become a ritual. They help me leave behind everything that's on my mind so I can focus properly on the task ahead. I would have to work hard that day. We were on the top floor of the hotel. Competing with the panoramic view to get any attention was going to be a challenge.

The hotel's Event Manager was eager to ensure I had everything I needed. One small detail bothered me. There were no wastepaper bins in the room. I'm not messy but, given that flipcharts and post-it notes are the tools of my trade, a bin is always welcome. Surprised at my question, the Manager looked back at me with a smile on her face. 'Sir, why do you need a bin when you have Jeff?' This is when I understood the role of the quiet gentleman who was by her side. He wasn't just assisting her with her checks. He was to be our go-to person for the week. His duties included picking up any litter we might have.

Jeff turned out to be delightful, funny, and incredibly efficient. Watching him, ashtray in hand, following delegates on a cigarette break, ready to catch any falling ash, was a sight to behold. You can buy any number of

DOI: 10.4324/9781032639390-11

books on customer service, but Jeff was a walking encyclopaedia of luxury hotel etiquette. He knew what I needed before I had thought of it myself.

He is the only reason I remember the conversation I had with my client over breakfast that morning. It's not that it was uninteresting or that I was uninterested. But it is a conversation I had had so many times before, and have had so many times since, that I could have easily forgotten the details. It was the contrast between Jeff and the content of our discussion that finally crystallised this new rule in my mind.

I had known my host for a long time. We had first met during a leadership development workshop. He was a middle manager on a course I was facilitating. Since then, his career progression had been stellar. I was still running workshops while he was now running the business. His life could not have been more of a contrast to Jeff's, yet he wasn't the one who looked satisfied. I asked him how he was getting on.

'To be honest with you, I'm pretty fed up. I used to enjoy the buzz, the doing, the selling stuff and getting stuck in. Now, my life is all politics. It's meeting after meeting, talking, chatting, and more meetings. It's so much blah blah blah. I just don't feel I do anything anymore.'

I'm not sure what Jeff would have made of someone who was paid so much to do seemingly so little being so unhappy! Yet, I knew exactly how my host felt and I was glad he felt this way because at least he was aware of the huge trap that faces anyone wanting to lead. This trap was one that only 'Rule 8 – Power up' could prevent him from falling into.

I have seen this situation so many times and I am sure you have too. The best salesperson becomes the worst sales director. The best finance person becomes the worst finance director. The best at anything becomes the worst leader of it. Let me explain why in the way I explained it in Hong Kong and show you how to avoid falling in the trap laid out for my client.

You may recall that in Rule 2 I said, 'At work, unlike in other areas of life, it is leaders, not followers, who appoint leaders.' This is the start of the explanation and lies at the root of the problem. Why would any leader promote anyone? The short answer is because they have spotted them. Why have they spotted them? Because they are the best at what they do. Whether in the public, private, or third sector, they get spotted in organisations because they do things better, faster, smarter, cheaper than others. They get spotted because they get results.

The more we do, the more results we get, the further we go. We get rewarded and promoted for doing. The more we achieve, the more we succeed. My client had been good at what he did. He was, by far, the best salesperson the company had and possibly had ever had. He was so good that he got promoted to manage a sales team. The team was made up of similarly driven and capable people.

So he continued to do what he was good at. He took his management job seriously. He got stuck in. He worked hard and got some big deals. Team members appreciated him. He was credible. They could learn from him. He could show them the ropes. Results were good so he was spotted again. In record time he went from managing a sales team to managing the sales function.

It is at this stage that someone should have told him about the trap that would eventually lead to his lack of enjoyment of his job and, more importantly for us, stand in the way of his success. He didn't know it, but this was his last chance to not fall into it. He was on the last promotion he could succeed at before he would have to change dramatically. He was reaching the inevitable point where the more he did, the less he would achieve. But no one was prepared to tell him the truth. He had been appointed because of his selling ability, yet, his new role required no selling.

But that's not how his leaders and he saw it. Rather, they saw leading as an accountability added to his sales role rather than a role in itself. So, my client did what he knew how to do and carried on selling. Now, though, he was selling for everyone. Remember, he was the best sales person. He took on key clients now that he was a key person. He got even more involved with his people.

He worked longer, harder, and achieved. His employees saw him as a great boss. At this stage it was still possible for him, just about, to manage. It was hard work. He felt he had to smash his target and everyone else's. But he did it. His bosses saw it and promoted him again. It was then that the trap became unavoidable.

My client was now in charge of the region. He looked after everything: marketing, sales, delivery, finance. He could no longer do everything. There was just too much to do for him to do it all himself. But he tried. That's why he saw meetings as distractions and discussions as politics. He had so much to do and so little time. He had to be on top of everything. He had fallen into the trap.

He was trying to go from being the best sales person to being the best sales, marketing, production, delivery, and finance person. He thought that being credible meant being the best at everything and being the best at everything was what made someone the best leader. I have seen this so many times that I have come to describe it as the 'FACE FACT stage' – the point when an executive goes from being Fast, Ambitious, Cerebral, and Engaged to Fast, Ambitious, Cerebral, but Tired.

He mistook his lack of achievement as resulting from a lack of capacity, rather than a focus on the wrong capability. He had mistaken what made him credible (his ability to be the best at something) for what would make him successful (his ability to ensure everyone else was the best they could be). He was so deep in the detail that he didn't just do other people's jobs rather than his: he tried to do everybody's job without understanding the nature of his own.

Over breakfast I told him to power up. I explained how organisational psychologists talk about two important drivers to career progression. I call these personal performance (i.e., achieving a personal target) and people-focused power (i.e., impacting and influencing others). The key to success is to understand that whilst we need both, the emphasis on each changes as our role evolves.

At the start of your career, it is your personal performance that gets you rewarded. You must achieve to advance. Often, as in my client's case, you may need some people-focused power to perform. He sold complex products that needed him to impact and influence his customers in order for them to buy. The trap is a failure to understand that the more you get promoted, in order to remain successful the more you need to trade personal performance for people-focused power. Your own discretionary effort is not enough. To succeed, leaders must create the conditions for others to release their discretionary effort. They can only do this through impact and influence. They can only win by using power.

The concept of power is often misunderstood in leadership. It has pejorative connotations. Much as my client did, power is often described as politics. It is seen as a game of influence, mainly for self-interest and aggrandisement. This is not what this rule is about. Understanding power means understanding the very essence of performance.

There are two different ways to exert power. The first is to feel big by making other people feel small. This is the type of power that leads to coercion. From a leadership standpoint it leaves you stuck with, at best, contractual effort. The kind of power I talked about that morning was different. It is the kind of power that leads to increased levels of trust and higher performance. It is the kind of power we value in our leaders.

When I arrived in the UK in 1985, the government was running an advert on TV to recruit teachers. The tagline was simple but effective: 'no one ever forgets a great teacher.' It always resonated with me because it is so true. Everyone I talk to remembers a great teacher. The same is true of leaders. Everyone can identify a great boss.

When you ask people why they remember these individuals in particular, you often realise that it is not because they are the people who made them laugh or made them happy. Instead, people never forget people who made them feel strong. We always remember those who made us feel more capable. These are the teachers and leaders who made you take a risk. They are the people who pushed you that little bit further than you thought it was possible for you to go. Sometimes it didn't feel right, and you felt nervous, but you knew they had your back. This is the right kind of power.

If there is such a thing as a silver bullet to ensure you succeed, this is it. Just ask yourself, every time you have an interaction with someone, 'Have I made them feel stronger and more capable?' If the answer is yes, they will follow you. Your role is neither to make people happy nor to make them deferential. Your role is to make them feel stronger and more capable. The word 'feel' is important as it's the outcome of your behaviour rather than just your intent that is important here.

When my son George wanted to learn to swim, we encountered the small difficulty that he really, really didn't want to get in the water. However great a teacher I like to think I am, this was an obstacle we struggled to overcome. Had I wanted to make George happy I would have given up right there. I knew he would cry. If I acted for performance alone, I could have just gone into the water myself and swum. This would have got the job of swimming done but it would have got George no closer to being able to take on this job. No amount of personal performance on my part could ever make him a swimmer.

I could have just pushed him into the water and told him that all would be fine. After all, I could have pointed out to him that I could already swim at his age, and he just had to trust me (and the lifeguard). He would have been scared. He would have probably panicked and may never have swum again. This is the wrong kind of power that I see too often, in too many organisations, exercised by too many leaders.

The right way to go about this is to do everything to ensure George feels stronger and more capable. He will still cry but I will be there. I will go down in the water with him. I have the credibility of my own swimming ability (i.e., my personal performance) to rely on, but I will need my people-focused power to impact and influence him. I will tell him I felt exactly as he did the first time I went in a pool when I was his age (that's empathy and it's a start). But compassion requires empathy to become active. It needs us to have a shared goal and some hope. So I will explain how, when he is able to swim, we will go far out in the sea. I will give him all the attention he needs to feel I have his back.

Power is not about avoiding making others accountable. On the contrary, making other people feel stronger and more capable is the only way we can get them to release their own motivation. Remember the three Cs from our last rule: choice, community, and competence? When we act with power, we can get others to make the right choice and show them that there is a community relying on and supporting their competence. Power is the engine of leadership.

Back in Hong Kong, following our breakfast conversation, I was rather impressed with the start of our meeting. Rather than the usual recap and debrief on actions taken, my client started with the four words from which all power flows: 'How can I help?' I'd like to say the week went incredibly well and that my client had changed dramatically in the space of one breakfast. It and he didn't. It wasn't an easy workshop. There were plenty of breaks when Jeff came up to me with a plate and a wink, whispering 'I think you need sugar for energy!'.

It was a tough week, but it was also a different week. Changing a lifetime of habits that are all associated with success is tough. But there is one thing that made it much easier – my client's thirst for performance. When someone has a lifetime of exceeding their targets you only have to set them a new one for power to watch them shine. Now, all he had to do was make sure everyone saw it. Our next rule was there to help.

From rule to lesson

Rule 8 – Power up

Careers are built on two drivers – personal performance and people-focused power. They are both necessary, but success requires an understanding of how the emphasis placed on each changes as we progress.

In the early stages of our progression, we get spotted for personal performance. The more we achieve the more we get promoted. We may be required to impact others to a greater or lesser extent depending on the nature of our role, but our primary responsibility is the achievement of our accountabilities.

When we eventually get promoted to a leadership role the emphasis changes. We reach a stage where, paradoxically, everything that has made us successful to date will get in the way of any future success. Rather than coming from 'doing', our success will now come from 'influencing'. This is why power matters.

The type of power that we need is not the kind that makes others feel small but, rather, it is the kind of power we remember experiencing from our best teachers and bosses. It is the kind of power we have when we can answer in the affirmative the key question, 'Have I made them feel stronger, and more capable?'

Rule 9

See and be seen

Warsaw, Poland

I have seen quite a few CEOs in hi-vis jackets. I have seen some wearing both hi-vis and hard hats. But the sledgehammer was a new one on me.

As far as symbolic gestures go, this one was rather grand. I had arrived in Warsaw to work with the newly appointed local CEO of an international organisation and his executive team. That morning, though, I would have to wait longer than usual for our meeting to start.

The CEO, surrounded by about 50 people, was busy smashing a wall in the staff cafeteria.

I knew I was safe. Our previous meeting had started with a risk assessment briefing by the Production Director. He had pointed out the odd cable we might trip over, along with the emergency exits. The company took health and safety very seriously. I was safe but no less shocked as the CEO, shirt sleeves rolled up, red from his efforts to bring down the wall, was shouting at the top of his voice 'you have to see and be seen'. This is our ninth rule.

I like to define culture as 'the way we do things around here'. It expresses itself through all the artefacts that make up an organisation. From the way we lead, communicate, and work to the buildings we inhabit and the hours we keep, culture is everywhere.

Up to that day, my client's canteen had been split in two. There was a large, functional, if somewhat impersonal, area for staff with an adjacent grand room for executives. One was called the refectory, the other the dining room. No wonder the senior leadership team was seen as aloof. The figurative distance employees felt from their leaders was a literal wall. The CEO wanted to break down the cultural barriers to success, so he decided to break down the partition to the dining room. He wanted the executive team to see and be seen.

The importance for leaders of seeing and being seen is not a new concept. It was popularised by two McKinsey consultants Tom Peters and Robert H. Waterman Jr in their 1980s blockbuster 'In Search of Excellence'. The

DOI: 10.4324/9781032639390-12

book was a global phenomenon. Arguably, it singlehandedly launched the business book category. Executives everywhere were picking up copies and working to apply its principles. One became particularly popular.

It came from Hewlett Packard, a relatively small American business at the time, certainly small relative to the giants the consultants were used to consulting with. Bill Hewlett and David Packard, who founded the company, took time to wander around their business. They wanted to talk and listen to their staff. They wanted to empower them to do their best work. They called this habit Managing By Wandering Around (MBWA).

But, as our 'Power up' rule tells us, executives don't much like the idea of wandering. It sounds rather unproductive. So they quickly changed the verb from wandering to walking. At least walking sounded more active. There is pace to walking. You can't wander fast, but you can walk fast.

Eventually, executives decided they had too much to do and not much time to do it in. Walking Around was dropped altogether and replaced by the Open-Door Policy. Sure, listening to staff views was important but staff could do the walking. The policy would also have the advantage of ensuring that only 'the important stuff' was discussed as no employee would waste their time coming to an executive's office unless the issue deserved a walk.

Executives quickly forgot the importance of presence and the impact it has on others. As Texas Bix Bender said and Tom Peters often quoted when discussing MBWA: 'A body can pretend to care, but they can't pretend to be there.' Employees weren't fooled.

By removing the wall, my sledgehammer-wielding CEO was not describing the activity of wandering but highlighting its purpose. The only point of MBWA, as he was chanting, is to see and be seen and when it comes to this, your open door might as well be shut. Proximity is the only way to exert the type of power we looked at in our previous rule. Wandering is not aimless. It is a deliberate strategy to make people stronger and more capable. This cannot be done remotely or passively. See and be seen is side-by-side action.

Having destroyed the best part of the wall (and his shirt in the process), the CEO asked everyone to sit down in the canteen to discuss why seeing and being seen mattered. Despite not being Polish himself, he was aware of the country's cultural norms and therefore the concerns his actions had created.

For many leaders, being distant is not about being superior. It is about appearing wise and knowledgeable. If you are there to make decisions and already know what is happening, you need a tranquil executive floor with its own dining room and you have no need to mingle to find out anything. Witness how, in open plan offices, leaders often require glass walls.

To avoid his senior team being on the defensive when it came to how they were perceived, the CEO decided to start the conversation discussing what they saw rather than how they were being seen.

By design the leader's role is a hierarchical remedial role. If the organisation is working properly the only issues that get escalated to the most senior levels are the issues that could not be resolved lower down the line. Communication is linear and focused on issues. If everything you see, and the only things you discuss, are problems, you end up seeing the organisation itself as a problem, and yourself as a problem solver. This flawed view of leadership and organisational reality quickly results in suboptimal results.

In the workplace, on any given day, most communications are conversations, and most conversations are asymmetric, amorphous, and focused on possibilities.

Think about it this way. If, as a parent, you spend your entire time spotting and correcting your children's mistakes, they will grow up knowing what to avoid without ever understanding what to do, repeat, and seek. If you want successful children, you will engage with them in conversations to discuss their success. You will try to make sense of the world together knowing that, when it comes to making them stronger and more capable, their experience of reality is as valid and important as yours. You cannot succeed just by fixing problems, you must also seize, and therefore see, opportunities.

The 'see' of 'See and be seen' is not about checking. It is not about spotting mistakes and errors. It is about having a rounded view of the organisation rather than a limited view of its issues. It is about finding out and recognising what works. It is about discovering what happens when things go well and having conversations about how successes can be leveraged. It is about seeking opportunities by having them jump out at you, rather than solving problems that have been brought to you. As we discussed in Rule 7, 'Only death demotivates', employees are more engaged when they feel supported and noticed.

To see is not just physical either. It goes beyond being there. Our CEO broke down the executive dining-room wall to underscore the mindset of 'See and be seen'. To see is about being able to recognise excellence and opportunities. It is about curiosity – a desire to find out what is going well and works. To see is about gathering the data that most leaders, driven by their deficit mindset, too often dismiss. This is the data that is everywhere for all who care to see: success data.

If 'to see' is the act of the leader towards her followers, 'to be seen' is its complementary opposite. You cannot 'power up' if you cannot be seen. You must be seen to have an impact. You must understand how you are seen to understand your impact. Our CEO wanted to make sure his leadership team understood that by removing themselves they left their impact to chance. By being less accessible physically, they were less accessible as leaders.

When leaders are seen, they become real human beings rather than remote problem solvers. This makes them less intimidating. Employees are more inclined to approach them to discuss their situation. Being seen also ensures immediacy in dealing with issues. It enables employees to benefit from a leader's expertise and experience and helps leaders to access the tacit knowledge resting in their employees.

Of course, the success, or otherwise, of 'See and be seen', like everything else at work and in life, rests in its implementation. Imagine being an employee of an organisation where leaders are aloof and constantly discussing problems. The canteen would be your solace. It would be the place you go to, to relax amongst colleagues, safe in the knowledge that no senior team members are looking over you. In this case, I don't think you would have rejoiced in seeing the wall come down.

Being physically present isn't enough. If employees are not used to seeing you around, if your culture has always been one of spotting mistakes and blaming people, if trust is low, 'See and be seen' will feel more like spying than caring. This is why we need to understand compassion and people-focused power before 'See and be seen' can work. Leaders must genuinely want to find out more and commit to doing something with others' concerns beyond dismissing them. With compassion and people-focused power, people will open up to you. Without both, you shut them down.

Being seen is beneficial only if you understand both your impact and other people's preferences. This is why 'See and be seen' are linked. You need to see to seek data and be seen to do something with it.

Your starting positions (i.e., how you are perceived), the cultural norms of the organisation (i.e., how things are done around here), and the personal preferences of individuals (i.e., what each is comfortable with) must dictate the nature of the actions you take. You will need to adapt your activities. Some may welcome you at their table whilst others would rather eat alone.

You will need to mind your body language as well as your actual language. You will need to make sure you see everything, not just what you want to see. You will need to listen twice as much as you talk and answer twice as much as you ask.

Breaking down a wall was symbolic. Symbols matter. But symbols alone don't change a culture. You need sustained courage, time, and hard work for that. After our morning meeting, when we all went down to lunch,

I heard the starting gun that started the culture change race. It sounded like laughter coming from a table.

One of the senior leaders, carrying his tray, approached a table where employees were deep in conversation. Fearing he was imposing himself and not wanting to disturb, he, rather apologetically, said 'just ignore me'. The reply 'we always do' coming from a burly employee and the ensuing laughter from the whole table, including the leader himself, told me that this 'See and be seen' idea might lead to something new.

The 'See and be seen' rule is a discipline. It requires attention and intention. It is necessary to keep others engaged in their work and you connected to yours. Leading is a contact sport. It is about being where the work is really being done alongside the people really doing it. Nothing should keep you from being there with them. It is not only critical to success but also fundamental to minimising the chances of failure described in our next rule.

From rule to lesson

Rule 9 – See and be seen

As I pointed out in our second rule 'Line up your screws', you are only a leader if others follow. If you turn around and find no one behind you, you are not leading anyone. To be a leader is therefore not something you can ever do alone, or be successful at, remotely. Leadership is all about relationships and relationships require seeing and being seen.

By seeing the world of work as it is, leaders can identify desirable processes, habits, and behaviours to replicate and amplify. They can recognise and reinforce success rather than just spot and correct mistakes. By being seen, they underscore their desire to be accessible and encourage communication. They increase their chance of being seen as trustworthy by displaying their humanity.

See and be seen can only succeed, as an activity, if you have mastered compassion as we talked about in Rule 6 'Empathy is grossly overrated'. Without compassion, it runs the risk of coming across as spying or judging. With it, a culture of openness and continuous improvement is created.

Rule 10

Mind the fresh paint

Prague, Czechia

The idea was for me to take the last flight out of London that evening. I was to spend the night in Prague. At 6 am the next morning, my client was to pick me up and and drive to the venue. We would inspect the facilities, make sure everything was as it should be, and drive back to the airport in time for me to be home for dinner.

It was a last-minute plan and, as with most last-minute plans, it was an expensive plan. I could get a discount on the hotel due to the last-minute booking, but that was never going to make up for the hefty increase on the price of my last-minute flight. I would be on the road for 24 hours to work for about one. Did it really make sense for me to get on that plane?

Of course, today the client could have simply video-called me from the venue on her smartphone and we could have talked it through. But this was 2002. We didn't have smartphones then (it would take another five years for the iPhone to appear and six for Android to be announced). And while video-conferencing was possible it wasn't the kind that worked on location, especially if that location was on the edge of a forest in rural Czechia.

Still, having stayed in countless 'business' hotels, in numerous countries, and knowing they all look pretty much the same, I am pretty sure there is only so much you can do with a conference room. If there are tables and chairs, all will be well. So why did my client want me there? The answer was simple. The meeting was a very big deal for her. She wanted reassurance. I did my job by pointing out that she didn't need it, but I also knew that my job was to make sure she was at her best on the day and that meant making sure she was at her best in the run-up to it too. So I got on the plane.

We were preparing the first off-site of a new executive team. Recently appointed, the CEO of this fast-moving consumer goods company (FMCG) had decided that he wanted some time with the senior team, away from everyday business pressures, to plan for the year ahead. I was there to give

DOI: 10.4324/9781032639390-13

feedback on how they worked as a team and offer some thoughts on how they might become more effective and quicker. It was an important meeting for all involved but, perhaps, even more so for my client who had just joined the company and had been asked to organise the event. She felt she had something to prove.

As is often the case when you take the last flight out of anywhere, my plane landed about two hours late. I discovered upon reaching the hotel, past midnight, that the night staff had assumed I wouldn't show up and had promptly resold my room. After much arguing it was decided that they would put me up in the presidential suite for the night. With about four hours left to go before my morning ride, I admit that I probably didn't show the expected gratefulness deemed commensurate with an upgrade from the cheapest to the most expensive room in the hotel. I am not always at my best when I am tired!

Here is a tip though for anyone who needs to de-stress after a hectic evening and too short a night. Have a drive through the Czech countryside the next morning. It is just beautiful. I can't tell you which part of the country we drove through, as I can't remember the name or location of the hotel. All I can recall is that there was a Skoda factory looming in the background as we travelled the last few kilometres to the venue. It might have provided much-needed employment, but it kind of spoiled the view!

Approaching the front desk, I could tell we were expected. The manager took great pride in telling me this was a historic hotel once used as a retreat by communist party apparatchiks. Judging from the rather risqué pictures on the bedroom walls and the numerous hunting trophies on display, I'm pretty sure they didn't make much use of the business centre.

As we walked through the facilities, everything looked just fine, as I suspected. We would be ok. But there was one thing that bothered my client. The hotel did not stock any of the company's products. Not one. She discussed this with the manager and a solution was easily found. She would ensure products were delivered to the hotel and the manager would ensure they were delivered to the relevant rooms.

She had found the perfect solution, and I had found the perfect way to start the meeting. I only had to make sure she was OK with me using this story as an example to shape an initial ground rule because I didn't want to embarrass her in any way. But this was too good a story and too important a rule to not be discussed. I call it the 'Mind the fresh paint' rule.

I am used to clients using their own products and services. Indeed, I make it a rule to use their products and services too! It seems only right. After all it would be weird if you didn't use your own stuff. Even my medtech clients try to find ways to experience what their users go through.

I am also used to my FMCG clients ensuring meetings are held at their suppliers' venues (you'll meet some of them later in the book). Again, it seems normal that if a hotelier goes to the trouble of stocking your products, you go to the trouble of staying at their place. Or if a restaurant stocks your drinks, you go there for your dinners. Indeed, my client had tried but, on this occasion, none of the hotels her company supplied could accommodate the meeting.

But our hotel manager understood that in the hospitality industry it's good to be hospitable and, if that meant stocking products he didn't normally stock, then so be it. The problem, in this case, did not rest in the solution but in the intent. It turned out that my client did not want anyone to raise the issue of the hotel not stocking their products. But why?

Was she fearful of the reaction of the top team? Was she wanting to protect the sales director from recrimination for not having managed to establish a presence in this establishment? Was she embarrassed she hadn't managed to host the meeting at a more suitable venue? When we discussed the matter on the drive back, she simply didn't know. The answer was along the lines of all the above and none of the above. She just didn't want it to be an issue. She wanted everything to be perfect.

This is the reason I called this rule 'Mind the fresh paint' because of a saying here in the United Kingdom. It's that 'the King thinks the country smells of fresh paint' because everywhere he goes, people have just finished repainting the walls. And so it is for leaders.

A CEO once shared with me his frustration at a driver who picked him up from the airport on a visit to one of his organisation's overseas operating companies. The chauffeur did not want to deviate from his planned route even though my client wanted a detour to a particular landmark which he had promised to photograph for his daughter. The driver was simply complying with the request of his local CEO who, it turned out, had booked every single billboard on the route to make sure the Group CEO would be reassured by the brand's presence in the country.

Similarly, a global finance executive told me of her frustrations at having travelled from London to review her operations in Australia, only to hear well-rehearsed presentation after well-rehearsed presentation. She eventually managed to ask a question only to get 'Shall I tell you honestly?' as the answer. As she put it, it was as though they thought she had flown for 23 hours to be entertained rather than informed.

Fresh paint is a perfume that all leaders wear.

Don't get me wrong. I am not telling you that employees are dishonest, duplicitous, or secretive by nature. Far from it. In my experience the fresh paint is applied to please. It is brushed on as a mark of respect. In the case of the CEO and his driver, the local team wanted him to be happy to see that they cared enough. The finance executive was being presented what the team thought she wanted in the most professional and succinct way possible, given her long journey. In the case of my Czech client, she just cared. In every case it was respect rather than fear of consequences that drove people's actions.

Whether designed to conceal dirt, mask cracks, or simply bring colour and light, fresh paint always hides the truth. Identifying intent is pretty much impossible, and assuming it counterproductive, especially when different cultures bring varied reasons for actions. Equally, we could never remove the need of others to protect their leaders from what they see as an unappealing reality, such as the absence of products at my client's chosen hotel.

When I eventually met the executive team on the edge of the forest near the Skoda factory, I told them about the fresh paint. They were impressed by my client's prompt action in ensuring products were available. They thought it thoughtful and proper. But they also thought both her actions and the absence of products at the hotel interesting. For them, neither was an issue. Both were data points.

The simple fact that this hotel did not stock their products and all the hotels who did were busy was data. It told them something about their segmentation, their pricing, and their brand image. That my client had decided to ensure product was available was data. It told them something about the engagement of employees with the brand, their attention to detail, and their need to please the executive team. Whether it told them something bad (to be embarrassed about and remedy) or something great (to be proud of and recognise) was irrelevant. Data, in and of itself, cannot be an issue. In fact, it is the absence of data that hides issues.

Getting to the truth is much harder than simply getting the truth. So, how do you create the conditions for the unpainted reality to be the default position in your business? In a way, it is not that different from getting anything else. You need to be clear and set standards by adopting three habits. Say it, show it, and stick with it.

Let's start with 'say it'. It seems obvious that for people to know what you want, you need to be clear and articulate it. You could go for something like 'I want us to be able to share everything' but the problem with this is that it can be taken quite literally. You can either get in trouble because people share things you wanted to keep confidential, or because you become inundated with information you really didn't need.

It is much better to be less specific on the outcome and more on the process. For example, the Czech executive team agreed to send the message that they wanted to see the world through the eyes of consumers, suppliers, and employees.

Saying something, though, doesn't always guarantee that it will happen, as people also must believe you mean it. This is where 'show it' comes in. There are two sides to showing it. The first is to role-model the behaviours you want to see. I am reminded of the CEO of a mobile telecommunications business who would bring to work the letters and bills his son and wife received from competitors. His point was that he wanted everyone to see what the competition was up to with customers, and the only way to do this was to be a customer. He role-modelled being outside the bubble.

That, however, is not enough. If you don't want to be sheltered from the truth you have to have enough self-control to react to it properly. Imagine if our executive team had kicked up a fuss with my client upon discovering the absence of their products in the hotel. You can guarantee it would have never happened again. Fresh paint would have been applied. People will only disclose issues if they know it is safe to do so. If your reaction to problems being voiced makes others afraid to voice them, you will always get 'no problem' everytime you ask a question. And that is when – as a leader I worked with used to say – ' "no problem" is a problem.'

If you want to see the world as it is you will need to depersonalise situations and remove emotions from discussions by making them data driven. Role-modelling what you want to see as well as encouraging it through your response is what 'show it' is all about.

Finally, we all have examples of leaders who have just come back from a course eager to make changes. We've all been there. We know they'll come back weird but eventually they settle down and go back to normal. Nothing in organisations lasts for long. The pendulum swings one way and then the next and clever employees just learn to duck.

It is for this reason that the last of our habits is 'stick with it'. The secret to avoiding the bubble is to burst it regularly. Some of my clients have regular meetings. One I particularly like is the 'best-kept-secret meeting' which, as the name implies, is a meeting at which people must disclose something about their function that is kept well hidden from people outside that function, something they do not wish other people to know. They then, as a group, work on solutions. It is a fun way to bring everyone around to a particular way of thinking. Symbols and traditions matter.

On their own, though, these kinds of meetings can quickly turn into gimmicks. Finding a daily habit is much more powerful and to my mind there is no better habit than asking the question my Hong Kong client had kicked off his meeting with: 'how can I help?' This simple phrase shows willingness to hear issues and openness to help – two things that unleash discretionary effort.

It is not easy to avoid the smell of fresh paint and too easy to get used to a nice clean room, but success comes from walking in other people's shoes, however smelly and worn they are. One thing is for sure, if you don't follow our next rule, it won't just be a room your employees have freshly painted. They will have erected an entire movie set.

From rule to lesson

Rule 10 – Mind the fresh paint

It is hard to remain connected to what is truly going on when so many others will inevitably show you what they think you want to see or tell you what they think you want to hear. People repaint the rooms the King visits not by virtue of who he is but by virtue of what he represents. What is true of the King is true of leaders.

To ensure you burst the inevitable bubble that so many leaders inhabit, there are three habits you must adopt.

The first is to say that you want to hear the truth. Stating that no problem is indeed a problem is useful. It lets people know that you view problems in the same way you view successes. They are both data points that facilitate learning.

But saying what you want is not enough: people must believe you. Doing what you say is much more powerful than just saying it. You need to show you mean it. Embrace the truth by exerting self-control when this truth is not the one you wanted to hear.

Finally, the hardest part will be to remember that staying connected to the truth is among the hardest of all leadership challenges. Find ways to challenge yourself and others to seek data beyond what is obvious and normal.

Rule 11

What gets measured never gets done

Home, England

Sometimes you don't have to travel very far to find a new rule. This time I didn't have to travel at all.

If you have children, then, at some stage, you will have the pocket money conversation. It may come as a question or, as was the case in our house, it could be a statement. That morning, just after breakfast, Charlotte, my eight-year-old daughter, looked at me, with the kind of serious look you reserve for a Bank Manager ahead of a tough negotiation, and said, 'Papa. I need pocket money.'

Note the use of the verb *to need*, rather than the, let's face it, much more appropriate *to want*. I guess she chose it to underscore the importance I should attach to the request. Let me also point out the use of the noun *Papa* which happened, to my great shame as it is entirely my fault, to be pretty much the only French she knew. I guess she chose it to underline the family bond which made this request impossible for me to ignore. She is now 25 and knows probably about ten more French words. I say probably as her Essex regional accent makes it very hard to make out what they might actually be.

Irrespective of when the ask comes, however, and in whatever language it is phrased, you won't be able to escape the pocket money conversation. Just don't handle it the way I did.

You see, normal parents always have a choice. Depending on their parenting philosophy and financial circumstances they can answer 'yes' or 'no'. I do not consider myself a normal parent. I am a leadership development professional. I believe in 'teaching moments'. When my daughter asks for pocket money, I think 'hmm, here is an opportunity for development'. So I decided that the act of giving pocket money could become a broader lesson about the value of personal contribution. I built an incentive scheme.

Using a page of flipchart paper, I wrote a table. For brushing her teeth every day, I would give Charlotte ten pence. For brushing her long hair

DOI: 10.4324/9781032639390-14

every day, I would give her 10 pence. For tidying her bedroom every day, I would give her 10 pence. For doing her homework I would give her 40 pence. Some might see this last target as a cultural move on the part of someone coming from a country often accused of putting education ahead of hygiene in its scale of priorities.

I explained the way the scheme worked, stuck the paper to the fridge, bought a packet of gold star stickers and waited for our first 'Payday Sunday'.

On Saturday I noticed that the week had gone rather well. Only the bedroom needed attention. I encouraged Charlotte to go and tidy it. She duly went. Fifteen minutes went by with not a sound in the house. I have two children. There is one thing every parent of multiple children knows. If fifteen minutes go by with no noise, something other than what you intended is going on.

I went to check. I opened the bedroom door. Nothing had been done. The bedroom was as untidy as it was earlier. Charlotte was lying on her bed. She was painting her nails, or rather colouring them with a marker pen. Mustering my best teaching voice, I asked for an explanation. 'Charlotte. We had a deal. You were going to tidy the bedroom. I was going to check it and then give you a gold star. We were going to be happy and tomorrow I was going to give your entire weekly pocket money earnings.' Charlotte looked back at me with what I, perhaps with a level of bias, would describe as the sweetest, prettiest eyes in the world and simply said 'Papa, I've been thinking. I think that for ten pence it's just not worth it.'

I guess she did learn a lesson. It is a useful business lesson. It was not the intended lesson, but it is a good one in the context of the extrinsic motivation we discussed earlier. For incentive schemes to work the reward must be commensurate with the perceived amount of effort required to complete the task measured. However, given that the rest of the scheme's requirements had been met that week, this certainly is not a lesson that deserves the status of a rule or the title I have given it. To understand why Rule 11 is titled 'what gets measured never gets done' we need to fast-forward to the following weekend.

That weekend we decided to go and visit Grandma and Grandpa. Having packed the car for the journey ahead, I proceeded to ask the children to get in it. 'Charlotte, George, come on, let's get in the car. We need to go see grandma and grandpa.' After a short but, given their satisfied faces, productive conversation between Charlotte and her younger non-swimming brother, George, they both appeared looking militant. My daughter (now shop steward) proceeded to the kitchen. She looked at the flipchart intently before declaring in an official-sounding voice, 'And how much is it for grandma and grandpa, because they're not on the flipchart?'

I was witnessing an unintended consequence of my efforts. In my desire to teach a lesson about values I had destroyed a broader focus on values. By bringing economic incentives into our lives, I had removed all forms of social and moral obligations. That's the important lesson and it lies at the heart of Rule 11.

To understand why what gets measured never gets done, we need to understand how organisations truly function. Any organisation (whether for profit or not) starts life as an idea or an ideal. The founder or founding members will get together to try to make the idea come alive. I like to call this stage 'the company stage' rather than the 'start-up phase'. I like the word 'company' for its Latin roots of breaking bread together as it underlines the work individuals do together to make sense of the future.

In a company everyone does whatever needs to be done to bring the idea to fruition. Roles and responsibilities matter but are easily put aside to get stuff done. The company is about a collection of individuals who bring their entire self to work and act because of moral and social obligations. In that sense it is like a family. Everyone knows the end goal and maintains contact through conversations.

In a company, measures are markers of progress. They tell us how close or how far we are to the goal. They inform us about how well or badly we are travelling on the road.

Eventually, though, as a company succeeds, it grows. When it grows it needs to get organised. It becomes an organisation. An organisation, unlike a company, cannot rely on individuals' goodwill occurring as a response to their social and moral obligations. It cannot get stuff done through endless contracting and conversations. It relies on clear roles, processes that inform rules, and economic incentives and consequences. Measures are no longer markers; they become targets. This is where our problems begin.

What my pocket money experiment illustrates is how poorly the company and the organisation coexist. The minute I put a monetary value on the items on the list of chores, the items took precedence over the intent. Charlotte wanted more money for the things she disliked most, and money for things outside the list of accountabilities. She was gaming the system rather fulfilling its purpose. Social and moral obligations took a backseat to the power of the economic incentive.

This is a well-known issue in social sciences and one that has been studied countless times in business. There is even a so-called law about it named after British economist Charles Goodhart who expressed the idea in an article way back in 1975. Goodhart law states that 'when a measure becomes a target, it ceases to be a good measure'.

As Charlotte so successfully demonstrated, targets and incentives lead to a narrow focus on immediate goals without considering the long-term consequences. Targets work. Charlotte will do whatever is on the flipchart provided the prize is worth her while. But targets work too well. She will *only* do what is on the flipchart. This means that to achieve anything, we need to anticipate everything. We need to be able to guess what we will need tomorrow and the day after.

By basing my targets and incentives on a few key performance indicators and metrics, I created a myopic view of what good social behaviour is. This is the reason employees prioritise achieving specific metrics, even when doing so is at the expense of other important aspects of the organisation's overall well-being.

By setting targets and incentives without considering potential unintended consequences, I created perverse outcomes. Charlotte might have been extreme in trying to monetise her grandparents, but many an employee will find ways to achieve their targets by manipulating the system, rather than focusing on the underlying purpose or value creation.

Measures and targets achieve exactly what they set out to achieve. They are insidious. They offer us a sense of comfort and false reassurance that progress is being made even when we might be going backwards. This is why this rule matters so much. There are two reasons why, despite appearances to the contrary, leadership success rests on an understanding that what gets measured never gets done.

The first is being very clear that the statement 'what gets measured gets done' is erroneous. It misses a critical step. In a company it is what gets talked about that gets done. The same is true in an organisation. It is still what gets talked about that gets done. The problem is that targets quickly become all we talk about. As a result, we no longer talk about how what measures represent and how they fit with the overall goal. We are clear about the measures but no longer clear enough about why they are there.

If you don't believe me, just think back to a time when you tried, or witnessed someone else try, to introduce a change in an organisation. You will have heard two statements that are taken as truisms rather than indicators of a deep dysfunction.

The first will have been 'change starts at the top'. I could go into a long explanation as to why this is false but a simple statement dear to many French people will suffice – 'it is never the King who starts the revolution.' The second statement is 'we need to include a target in people's key performance indicators'. This is the 'how much is it for grandma and grandpa' statement. If it's not on the flipchart it won't happen.

As leaders, we need to make sure we discuss measures in their context. Clarity does not come from a sole focus on measures and roles. It comes from knowing how these measures and roles fit within the overall goal we set ourselves. Otherwise, measures will restrict any form of discretionary effort and innovation.

The second reason why leadership success rests on understanding 'what gets measured never gets done' is that measures, by disconnecting the company from the organisation, blind us to the overall purpose we set out to fulfil. Measures create a reversal. They ensure that an organisation flips from a purpose searching for assets, as it was in its infancy, to an asset searching for a purpose.

By disconnecting the company, measures disconnect us from the dynamism and adaptability brought about by 'people trying to make sense of the world together'. Instead, measures encourage counterproductive competition between teams along with tunnel vision on the part of employees.

Successful leaders require dynamic organisations. This can only be achieved if others are trusted to deliver, with measures that serve as reminders of standards rather than replacement goals. Constant and consistent conversations around what matters are what matters.

My problem was not that I devised an incentive scheme. It is that I talked about the measures without reminding Charlotte of their importance in a broader frame. It only mattered that the bedroom was tidy because it showed we were all in this together and we did not take anyone in our family for granted. I wanted her to complete tasks that reinforced our moral obligations. By measuring the tasks, I had broken the moral obligations. What got measured only got done when we started to talk about the value of grandparents beyond a present or future return on time invested in them. That was a fun conversation.

That's not to say that money doesn't matter, as we will see in our next rule.

From rule to lesson

Rule 11 – What gets measured never gets done

As organisations grow, measures multiply. They are necessary as tools to inform us of what is going on in a system grown too complex to be understood solely through observation and conversation. Measures help us simplify.

The problem starts when measures either replace conversations or become the only topic of conversation. They are no longer markers of progress towards a desired end goal but become, instead, an end in themselves. That is, the measure takes precedent over what we aimed to measure.

While measures matter to set standards and monitor progress, we can only lead if we have conversations about why they matter and what they inform. This will ensure measures are used for the positive achievement of organisational goals rather than being something to be gamed for the benefit of individuals.

What gets measured never gets done; rather, it is always what gets talked about that gets done. Success lies in ensuring measures are not the only things that get talked about.

Rule 12

Follow the money, not the fashion

Athens, Greece

As a purveyor of leadership development workshops, I am pained to say this, but I think more value is typically added during the breaks in a workshop than during the workshop itself. It is often over coffee that participants become individuals again and make valuable connections. Today, though, it was after a workshop had finished that valuable connections were made.

Katherine (my co-director, sometimes co-author, then fiancée, and now wife) and I were in Greece to co-facilitate a workshop. On our last night in the country, we decided to explore the city that, after a week, we had yet to discover. It was the light coming from the display of hundreds of colourful lit-up spirit bottles that attracted us to Brettos wine bar situated in the shadow of the Acropolis in the Plaka district of Athens. But it was the wine list and the elderly bartender that ensured we stayed the evening.

I am from Burgundy. By rights I should know a lot about wine. But I don't! I can tell white from red but I'm not even sure I would do so in a blind tasting. Katherine is from England; by rights, she should know nothing about wine. Yet, she does! In fact, she is quite the expert. On top of knowing the difference between red and white, she will tell you the grape, the country, and maybe even the vintage in a blind tasting.

The Greeks also know a lot about wine. They've been making it for a long time. In fact, they like their wines so much that they tend to keep the best ones for themselves. Today, it is still hard to find Greek wines in the UK. Back then, it was nearly impossible. That's why Brettos was such a good find. Having survived two world wars, one civil war, and a dictatorship, Athens' oldest bar and distillery is as famous for its Greek wine collection as it is for its homemade spirits.

The bartender and Katherine hit it off immediately. Wine people like talking to other wine people. I guess it's because most people tend to move on to other topics after an hour of discussing wines. The old man gave us a couple of samples before disappearing down to his cellar. He emerged after

DOI: 10.4324/9781032639390-15

a short while holding a few more bottles and a plate of Kefalotyri cheese. He carried on pouring, encouraging us to help ourselves to the cheese.

After a while, I pointed out that we hadn't yet paid for anything. His reply became our rule. 'Don't worry. You don't pay anything. This is all my gift to you. My job is to talk to you and find out information. I choose wines that match the information. You taste them and you will find one that is just perfect for you. Then you will want to buy many bottles to take away and you will want to come back. You are happy and I make money.'

He was right. We did buy two bottles (rather pricey by my standards and 'a bargain' by Katherine's) and although I can't pretend to be an 'influencer', I ended up giving him rather a lot of free advertising. I have mentioned Brettos to numerous people in countless speeches over many years. He did indeed get more in return than he spent on the six tasting samples and cheese plate he gave us.

Many people like to make business sound complicated. Our host made it sound simple. He showed us how, at core, all business models follow a similar template (although some may be inherently more complex than others). Whether through intuition, education, experience, or all of them, our host was a master of its application. The template rests on the fact that the cornerstones of any organisation are the four Cs – Customer, Cash, Change, and Capital.

Before you decide to skip this rule if you work in the public or the not-for-profit sector, know that these four apply to you too. You may have service users rather than customers and, if you work to alleviate poverty, for example, you may want to have fewer rather than more service users, but your raison d'être is still to serve them. You may not work to increase cash, but you will still need some to operate. You may not want to grow your organisation, but you will still need to change it to adapt. And regardless of what you do, your success will always depend on providing the best return on any capital invested in your endeavour. The four Cs are everyone's foundations.

Let's start with customers. The more you know them, the more you can tailor your proposition, the more satisfied they are, and the more successful you will be. As our host explained to us, knowing and understanding your customers so that you can offer the perfect solution to their needs is the best way to ensure you become their provider of choice for the service or product they seek.

Whether you are targeted to grow revenue (what you get in), reduce cost (what you pay out), increase profit (the difference between what you get in and what you paid out), or EBIT or EBITDA (ask an accountant friend because everyone calculates that one slightly differently), you should know that none of these will ever buy you a drink. Cash is the only currency that matters in Brettos and the only one that guarantees your existence every-where else. Every other measure is just an intermediary.

Cash is the blood that runs through the organisation. Understanding how cash flows through your organisation is understanding what keeps it alive. You only generate cash when it hits your till. An invoice is worth nothing until it is paid, and you won't have suppliers for long unless you pay them. Same for a non-profit: donors can make promises, but you can't provide services with promises alone.

Our host had explained customer and cash well. He invested some of his wine and cheese in getting to know us so that we would spend as much of our disposable cash as possible with him. So far, so simple. But, whilst customers and cash make Brettos a successful bar, it is change and capital, our next two building-blocks, that have made it the oldest one in Athens.

Many business consultants will tell you about the importance of growth. The problem with growth is that it carries the assumption that bigger is always better. Expanding Brettos or franchising its model does not guar-antee a better business. The owners would need to invest to ensure bar-tenders are all as good as the ones they currently have. In so doing they might take their eyes off the original bar. Growing offers opportunities but does not guarantee success. Changing, however, guarantees survival.

Customers change. Competitors, sectors, and environments change. Fail to keep up and you fall into irrelevance. You may not want to grow but you will always need to change. To matter, change has to be sustainable. It needs to improve both your revenue (the money that comes in) as well as your profit (the money that's left after you've paid what you owe). Without our last C, capital, however, what sounds logical is far from easy.

Think of capital as the cash you invest in your business. It is needed for your operation to continue as it is and to adapt as necessary. It might come from you, or you might borrow it from others. Success depends on getting more return from the capital you invest than you would have got from keeping it. If you borrow $10 from a bank at an interest rate of 10% to lend it to someone else at an interest rate of 5% you are a good friend but a poor investor.

Giving $10 worth of free wine to get $100 back in sales sounds like a pretty good idea. But unless you know the cost of the wine, how much interest you pay on the money you borrowed to buy it, how much interest you would have got by leaving the money in the bank and how much more you could have made by investing it elsewhere, you'll never really know. Understanding return on capital is the only way to make good decisions.

The problem for us is that, unless you work somewhere like Brittos, get-ting an overview of the four Cs is hard. It is easier to get to know your cus-tomers when you can speak to them directly. It is easier to understand cash when you see it come in and go out on daily basis. It is easier to change your organisation when you have a 360 degree view of it. It is easier to see if you are getting the right return on your capital investment when you are the only one dealing with the bank.

When organisations grow, they become harder to understand. As we saw in our previous rule, they get fragmented, become complex, disconnected, and siloed. The bigger or more complex the organisation gets, the more specialised people become and the more compartmentalised our four Cs are.

Few employees directly interact with customers and consumers. Cash gets translated into a revenue or profit budget that employees are accountable for delivering. Change is compartmentalised and divided into projects that only impact a small part of the overall value to customers. Return on capital is divided into a set of measures that are only aggregated back inside the finance department.

The more efficient organisations become, the more disconnected employees are from the four Cs. To solve this, organisations turn to fads. Every new initiative that organisations launch, every new concept that consultants sell, and every new system employees are trained to use has one aim: reconnecting the organisation. They are all designed to bring intimacy back into an efficient business.

Whether it is reengineering, six sigma, 'agile', customer experience, design thinking, digitalisation, or any other you care to mention, each and every one of them has been adopted in the hope that the organisation could be unified again. They have been designed to make the big feel small. They exist to help employees be as intimate with the four Cs framework as they are efficient in delivering parts of it.

This is both a legitimate and a desirable endeavour. We cannot succeed without an appreciation of how our effort contributes to the overall outcome. We cannot make the right decisions for our organisation unless we understand it in its entirety. The problem is not the aim but the method. As we saw in our last rule, it is what gets talked about, not what gets measured, that gets done. When fads take hold, they become all we talk about. They become the focus.

Organisations only succeed if they are differentiated by learning faster than the rate of change and their competitors – and so do individuals. Brettos' bartenders are few and far between. Regardless of their field, it is their command of the four Cs, not their grasp of the latest fad, that differentiates them. This does not mean that you need to become an accountant and/or teach everyone around you accounting. Finance may well be the language of business but not everyone has the ability, the interest, or indeed the patience to become fluent in it.

Instead, your task is to ensure you can translate the four Cs into a unified view of your organisation that resonates for all. Finance is simply a representation of this. It is a mirror showing us what we truly look like. Success, in any endeavour, comes from understanding reality. The four Cs are the only true cross-functional performance indicators that an organisation has.

If we can't clearly explain our role in the delivery of a differentiated experience for customers, either we don't understand our job or maybe we don't actually have a proper one. And don't try to get away with suggesting your customers are 'internal customers'. This is lazy. 'Internal customers' shouldn't exist. They only block your line of sight to 'end customers'. Your task is to determine clearly the contribution your function makes to both understanding your end customers and differentiating the offers you make to them.

If we can't identify the actions we can take to help cash flow better, or improve our return on capital invested, we don't have a sufficient grasp of how our role fits inside our organisation. Even if your division (note how even the word suggests the organisation is disconnected) is not incentivised directly to generate cash, do you know how you can help with cash flow or costs? Maybe you can reduce your inventory or agree better payment terms? Make a friend in finance and ask them!

If we don't understand how our change efforts impact our cash as well as our attractiveness, maybe we shouldn't propose them. Is what we want to do increasing our profitability (in terms of benefits returned for time invested if a not-for-profit)? Is it helping us differentiate? Use the four Cs as a way to explain the purpose of your initiatives. Only if you can positively influence all four will the initiative be worth the organisation's while.

Customers don't care how complex you are. Your donors or lenders don't care how tough your environment is. Your competitors won't stop competing just because you are struggling. Business can be tough, it can even be complex, but at its core it should never be complicated.

'Follow the money, not the fashion' is a call to action not to be blinded by the latest model, fashion, system, or process. It is a reminder that all exist for the purpose of making you better at delivering against the four Cs. You can only succeed if you grasp the fundamentals of your organisation and focus all your resources on them.

You will not be differentiated by your grasp of the numbers alone but without it you cannot be credible.

At the risk of giving the impression that I spend more time drinking than is good for my health, it was in another bar, some 3000 miles away, that our next rule was formulated. It is one that will help you understand the symbiotic relationship between you and your stakeholders: how you can only succeed in mastering the four Cs when you help them manage theirs.

From rule to lesson

Rule 12 – Follow the money, not the fashion

Although some business models are more complex than others, all organisations, regardless of their sectors, are built on four corner-stones: customers, cash, change, and capital.

We must understand our customers and why they choose us over alternatives. We need to know how cash flows through our organisation. We have to be proactive in changing to keep up with the changes in the environment within which we operate. We have to understand how the decisions we take impact the return we ultimately achieve.

As we endeavour to make our organisations simpler, more connected, and agile, we will invariably be drawn to use new tools, models, processes, and structures. Yet, regardless of which we choose, we must remember that our primary focus has to remain on the corner-stones of value rather than the attraction of a fad which will, eventually, be replaced by another.

Rule 13

Everybody wins, or nobody wins

New Delhi, India

It is in India that I found balance.

But don't worry. I'm not about to take a 'self-help yogic guru' turn. I didn't go to India to find myself, or anything else for that matter. I went there with a multinational group of senior leaders who wanted to learn more about their fastest-growing yet most challenging market. After a day of fact-finding visits and conversations our host decided to show us a different side of the country.

To say that India is a place of extremes and contrasts won't win any travel-writing prizes. But seeing a gleaming new shopping mall by a three-lane road turned into a six-lane highway by the ever-inventive Indian drivers was unexpected.

If you managed to ignore the surrounding noises and smells, the cars, lorries, motorbikes, the tuk-tuks, pedestrians, and assorted animals all trying to coexist on the road, you could have been in any metropolis in the world. By the time we parked, entered the sports bar chosen for our meal, spotted the football memorabilia, and perused the menu, we were in the US!

When they get together, middle-aged people can be boring dinner guests. I should know, I am one. So, the conversation turned back to business and the bar owner joined us to discuss his. It is his phrase that is our thirteenth rule.

'My rule when setting up this business was "everybody wins, or nobody wins". We all must make a little. If I make too much my customers must pay more. They end up with less. If my suppliers charge me too much, I either make less or charge more. They win but either I lose, or my customers lose. The key to my business is that we all win. I make a little, my suppliers make a little, my customers only pay a little. A little, plus a little, plus a little equal a lot for all of us.'

My friend Shaun O'Callaghan, founder of Quartet Research, and Head of Restructuring at Grant Thornton, calls this balancing your wobble board.

DOI: 10.4324/9781032639390-16

A wobble board is a simple piece of gym equipment. Think of it as a circular board with half a football underneath. The aim of the wobble board is to help athletes build their core strength by learning to balance on the unsteady platform.

In the context of business, we all stand on a wobble board. Every business has demands made on it by several constituencies. Each of these has different needs. The finance community made up of owners, shareholders, analysts, lenders, or taxpayers and donors if you work in government or non-profit, has demands and needs. The customers/consumers of your products and services have demands and needs. Your suppliers (also including the people who supply your license to operate such as regulators, NGOs, journalists, etc.) have demands and needs. The employees have demands and needs.

It doesn't even matter where you sit in an organisation. Everyone has a wobble board. As we saw in our last rule, you may be removed from direct contact with any, or indeed all, of these constituencies, but whether through budgets or targets, their demands still impact your actions.

At any point, each constituency can change its demands and needs and, to complicate matters further, the demands from one may contradict the needs of another. Your customers may well want your product for free, but your employees and suppliers will demand payment. Your suppliers will want to be paid on delivery but your financiers will want you to manage your cashflow by delaying your payments to suppliers.

But the rule is not just 'everybody wins' – it also states 'or nobody wins'. The demands made by different constituencies may be opposite, but they are co-dependent. It is only by meeting one that the other one can be met. You may be able to get away with pleasing one constituency for a while while disregarding the needs of another but if one loses, they will unbalance your board to the point that everyone falls off. It is only a matter of time.

As demands change within constituencies and interactions between them evolve, you might assume that your knowledge of stakeholders and practice in balancing would make life easier. That would be true if it weren't for context. Context always comes along to kick your board or change it entirely. Crises happen. You can never be comfortable on a wobble board.

Put your all weight on one side, and you risk falling off. Ignore one corner of the board and the forces impacting it become unmanageable. Building your core strength is hard enough. Having to put up with relentless kicks to the board from stakeholders is tiresome enough. Having to do both can feel overwhelmingly impossible.

So, what is the rule?

'Everybody wins, or nobody wins' is all about implications. It implies that to succeed you need to understand your board, your context, and your strength.

Our Indian business owner understands his board. His target customers are affluent young professionals who enjoy a beer and food after work. The mall needs his rent and his customers. His suppliers need his sales. His employees need the place to be full, so they get wages and tips. He understands the levers of supply and demand as well as the four Cs discussed in our last rule.

He understands his context. He knows what he has. He has a bar. It is a nice bar. With its American theme, it is a differentiated bar. But he is also honest with himself. He knows that there are plenty of other establishments for his customers to choose from. Some are even in the same mall. He also knows that his bar is dependent on the local economy remaining buoyant and the appeal of a 'Westernised' experience remaining strong. His is a local bar at the mercy of global geopolitical trends.

He also understands his strength. His offer is balanced. He offers an American sports bar atmosphere with fair pricing for good food and fashionable drinks. It is a typical afterwork spot in an atypical spot. It brings an image of America at an Indian price point. His food and beverage offer isn't unique. He doesn't want it, nor does he need it, to be. He just needs it to be good. That is the point of the bar. It's a good bar. Everybody wins.

Understanding your board, your context, and your strength means that the rule does not limit choices. It informs actions.

Let's say our bar owner decides to double the price of his food. Can he? Of course he can. But he can only do so successfully if he remembers the rule. If everything else remains the same, his board is unbalanced. He wins but customers lose.

If his were the only American bar in Delhi and customers were desperate for the experience, then things might be different. A unique product developed by a unique company offers a 'monopoly'. This gives you options on the board. But you need to understand your strength. In this case you are only as good as you are unique and, in this space, monopolies are only either temporary or unbalanced.

The mistake is to assume that the board is all about numbers. It is true that cash is the only variable common to all constituencies on your board. It is the only value they share, but it is not the only value they have.

If it was only about cash no one would ever buy a Rolex rather than a cheap watch to tell the time, nor would anyone ever want to go to an American bar in a shopping mall in Delhi rather than to a food truck outside it to eat.

The board is about the values we hold as well as the value we get. There are two forces at play for everyone to win. Let's call them shareholder equity and personal equity.

Even though the term shareholder won't represent the financial community on every wobbleboard (you may not have any shareholders in your organisation), I use it to describe everyone. In the context of the wobbleboard everyone has equity in the business. Everyone owns a share. For them to win, their share must be worth something. That is the reward side of 'everybody wins'.

The financial community makes a return (or allocates spending in the wisest possible way in the case of not-for-profit and governmental agencies). Suppliers and employees get paid. Customers and consumers get a service or product they want. The reward doesn't have to be financial. It can be about status, as in the case of the Rolex watch, or style as with our bar. It can be about an experience that enriches your life as in, arguably, both of these examples.

Whatever the nature of the reward is, there must be one for everyone to win.

But what of personal equity? I use the term personal equity to describe the need for everyone to feel they have their 'fair share'. As human beings, irrespective of the role we play in any transaction, we aim to be treated fairly. We don't want to feel we have been 'done'.

No one likes to be a schmuck, feel like a mark or a victim. No one wants to feel they have been cheated. This is not so much about personal gain as personal equity. Were we treated as fairly as others? Think about the last time you waited patiently in a traffic jam to come off the motorway only to see a car drive fast on the outer lane and pull back at the last minute in front of everyone. Maybe you were even the car letting the driver pull in front of you. You had that 'yeah right' thought in your head as the driver gave you a little wave to thank you for being a schmuck!

You put up with it on a road because you don't have a choice. You feel a sense of injustice in the smugness of others and maybe even disappointment in your own need to obey the rules of politeness. One thing is for sure, though: these are not feelings you enjoy. You may never become the unruly driver, but you will do whatever you can to avoid that feeling again. In business terms, it means the end of a relationship. Personal equity, fairness, and justice matter in any relationship if it is to last.

For everyone to win, not only does everyone need to have the feeling they have won, but also the feeling that others haven't won at their expense (financially or otherwise). Balancing the board is about value and values. It is about economics and psychology.

There is one last important issue with Rule 13 and the wobble board in general which I have yet to address. In a world where the demands of one constituency contradict the needs of another, how do you meet all of them? How can everyone be happy when their demands conflict? How do you deal with 'either/ors' when both those on the one hand and on the other need to be fulfilled? This is where Rule 14 for success comes in.

From rule to lesson

Rule 13 – Everybody wins, or nobody wins

So, what can we learn from Rule 13? Success comes from relationships. In any organisation, relationships are multiple and multifaceted. If you want to be successful in your endeavours, you need to balance the needs of all your stakeholders. They must all feel that they have won without ever feeling that they have had to compromise to accommodate the greater gain of others.

To even have a chance of achieving this kind of outcome you must understand your stakeholders (their pecuniary as well as psychological needs), your context (the economy, the market, the environment, the trends you operate under), as well as yourself (your strengths, your weaknesses, and your ability to change both).

You can always win in the short term by making others lose. As we saw with power, you can be stronger by making others weaker, but the only sustainable strategy is to win by making others stronger. As one self-effacing and relentlessly successful Indian entrepreneur would say, 'Everybody wins, or nobody wins.'

Rule 14

'Both' is the only answer to 'either/or' questions

Copenhagen, Denmark

If population size is what gives a country its impact, then Denmark punches above its weight.

From a business standpoint it is a country that accompanies us from cradle to grave. We play Lego as children and drink a glass of Carlsberg with friends as young adults. NovoNordisk's medicines ensure we grow old, whilst Coloplast's products help us do so with dignity. Maersk's ships and containers transport our goods throughout the world.

Wealthy readers might be perusing these lines through their Lindberg glasses, sipping a drink out a Georg Jensen glass, held tightly in their Pandora-bejewelled hand, with muted tunes emanating from their Bang and Olufsen speakers.

Anyway, you get the point. When it comes to being there for us, Denmark's brands are no fair-weather friends. They are everywhere. A capitalist country, with one of the most advanced social systems in the world and a population at once self-deprecating and proud, the Kingdom of Demark manages to rank as both the world's best country to live in and one of its happiest.

But that morning, the small, overcrowded room overlooking a typically pristine, bike-filled Copenhagen street sure didn't feel like the best place to be. If happiness is closely linked to social equality and community spirit, I was witnessing a particular situation – namely, marketing and production professionals gathered in the same room at the same time – that could break both. It had started well enough with a coffee and the inimitable Danish pastries, but once pleasantries had been exchanged the teams got down to business.

They had come together to agree on a way forward and I had come to help facilitate the conversation (although 'referee' would have been a better description). I don't need to name the company as the issue is universal and you will be familiar with it. We have already discussed issues arising

DOI: 10.4324/9781032639390-17

from targets and incentives in previous rules, and no targets/incentives are more opposed than those applied to marketing and production.

Whatever the metric used, marketers' targets are always linked to market penetration. As a result, they aim for what we described earlier, in Rule 12, as intimacy. They identify multiple segments, for which they need multiple channels and products to 'personalise' their offer. For production people, efficiency takes precedence over intimacy. They are focused on eliminating complexity. Cost minimisation is in their DNA.

Marketing people try to explain to those backwards 'couldn't-sell-anything-even-if-they-could-communicate' production folks the needs of the market, whilst business-minded, analytical production people try to rein in those fancy 'know-nothing-but-pretend-they-do' marketing types, who clearly have no care in the world for costs and think a product is a PowerPoint slide coming out of a printer.

Replace the insults and invectives with ones that suit whatever departments you have in mind, but you always come to the same conclusions. The world of organisations is a world of dilemmas best described as 'on the one hand, on the other hand' propositions where both positions are equally desirable.

Marketing (or sales) and production are extreme representations of what business author Art Kleiner calls the clash of a culture of hype with a culture of craft but what is true of these two departments is true of everyone. Every department in every organisation has a counterpoint with a focus and a target seemingly opposed to their own. Put any of them in a room together and you have my meeting.

In my experience, these meetings simply plough on until everyone realizes they are going to be late for their next meeting, so a compromise is found halfway between the needs of the marketers and the demands of production. No one is happy but, at least, everyone is relieved and released. Until, that is, the next meeting.

Things were different this time, as halfway through the meeting, a senior executive entered the room. Having listened in on the conversation, she was confronted by one of the participants. His question was simple, 'On the one hand, we in marketing are targeted to deliver X. On the other, they in production are targeted to deliver Y. The two are opposite. You can either have X or Y. So, which do you want? Which is more important to you?'

Her answer became our rule. As you might suspect, she said, 'I want both. I want both because we need both.' Furthermore, she added, 'We set your targets not to pit you against each other but to clarify your expertise and underline that as experts in each of your disciplines, only you can come up with the solution to what "both" looks like.' If she'd added 'so now back to work' it would have sounded like a Hollywood script!

To those in the room, having already endured an hour's worth of difficult conversations, this sounded both unreasonable and borderline deluded. But to anyone who wants to be successful it is a call to action.

Wanting both is not the same as wanting half of each. Wanting both is not the same as wanting some of one now and some of the other later. Wanting both is simply wanting success. 'Both' is the only possible answer to 'either/or' questions. That's our Rule 14.

But let's think about this in practical terms rather than abstract models. What was our senior executive saying when she told the room she wanted both? She was simply pointing out that to be successful their business had to attract the maximum number of customers with the minimum product cost. To say 'let's have the maximum number of customers and damn the cost' won't balance our wobble board for long. Neither will incurring so little cost that our product appeals to no one.

The problem for our marketing and production teams is that they weren't thinking about what both could look like. They were only thinking about X and Y as opposites. This is why consultants love two-by-two matrices and why the right answer is always in the top right-hand corner.

If you think about X and Y as opposites on a line, the middle is the only solution to the conundrum of wanting both. If they are extremes, they cannot possibly meet. Your solution will always be an average by nature and a compromise by default. A compromise cannot satisfy either requirement.

But if you think of X and Y as axes on a two-by-two, regardless of whether you have a business degree, you know that the logical answer is the top right corner. It is the optimum. You want the whole of X and all of Y.

It is also where innovation lies. Innovation is simply what other people haven't been able to think about because they have been too busy thinking about compromise. As a result, many businesses end up producing mediocre products. They averagely appeal at an average cost. They are compromise products and services for people who are compromising, and these people will stop compromising as soon as a better alternative comes along.

But what is the solution? In my experience businesses are stuffed full of clever people doing their best to do well for the business as well as themselves. So why is thinking about 'both' so hard and coming up with a solution so impossible for so many?

My friend and global authority on culture, Fons Trompenaars, has spent his life studying dilemmas. His seminal work in this field is worth several books (never mind a chapter in mine) and luckily for us he has written many. In essence he ascribes our difficulty in reconciling opposites to our cultural norms. Culture is our way of getting rid of dilemmas. It is therefore no wonder that when we get together with people with different work cultures, nationalities, backgrounds, etc. we find it hard to see beyond our own extremes.

Getting to a 'both' solution requires us somehow to remove the emotional and cultural biases underpinning our conversation. Success demands a new form of dialogue.

Let me give you an example to illustrate how we can move beyond what Fons calls 'OOH-OOH propositions' ('On the One Hand, On the Other Hand'). I want this example to be as far away from business as possible so as not to get caught up by any preconceptions you or I might have.

When Katherine and I decided to get married, as couples do, we planned a honeymoon. We are both lucky to have visited countless countries and cities during our careers. There is however one city that is dear to us both – New York.

Katherine has lived in New York. We got engaged in New York. Whenever we get the chance, we cross the Atlantic to stay in our favourite hotel, visit our favourite spots and restaurants, and just walk endlessly through a city we love. But, although New York seemed the logical choice, a honeymoon should be a special trip where we would get the chance to discover something new.

There is a country neither of us has visited. That country is Japan. Japan seemed ideal. It was a country we could discover together – do something truly new. There was a risk that we ended up disliking it but, in a way, taking risks is what makes life fun; Japan could have been just the place for our honeymoon.

So, on the one hand we could go to New York where we were guaranteed an amazing time and on the other hand we could go to Japan where we were guaranteed something new. What were we to do?

Adopting our marketing and productions teams' methodology would have meant us looking at a map. All the way to the left is New York, all the way to the right is Japan. Our executives will look for a compromise. They will seek the average. They will try to phase it. Maybe a bit of time in New York and a bit of time in Japan could have been the answer. Not only would this have made our honeymoon unaffordable, but it would also have guaranteed neither destination would be fully explored.

Or they will opt for the middle and end up in Istanbul. Now don't misunderstand me. There is nothing wrong with Istanbul. It is a wonderful city full of wonderful sights and wonderful people. Yet, it would have been a compromise. It fulfils none of the requirements of NYC or Japan.

The problem is that we are still thinking in terms of either/or. We are thinking in terms of solutions to our dilemma rather than trying to understand why we are in the dilemma in the first place. To move away from our biases, we need to list the positives and negatives of both extremes (in our case both destinations). We can then use these to see how we can maximise the positives on both sides.

Just to keep it simple, what Katherine and I could agree on is that we wanted a honeymoon we were guaranteed we were going to like. It needed to be familiar and to remind us of our shared past experiences. It also needed to be an adventure and be exciting by virtue of being different from anything we had ever done.

By going back to positives and negatives of the two extremes we are moving away from them. We now understand what 'both' means. Of course, in the process of listing positives and negatives for each extreme you might end up with one side overwhelmingly positive and the other mainly negative. That's ok, provided you have done your job correctly by being courageous and objective in coming up with the list. All it means is that you don't have a dilemma; instead, you have a decision that has just made itself for you.

But if, as it should be, the lists are pretty much equal then you have changed the question. In our honeymoon example, the question was no longer 'do we opt for something romantically familiar or differently adventurous?' but rather 'how can something familiar be different and how can something romantic be adventurous?'.

So, what is the right answer? There was something neither of us had ever done and which felt like an adventure with the right destination outcome. Neither of us had done an Atlantic crossing before. We're not talking about those crazy sailing or rowing crossings that sports people do. That's not the kind of adventure we had in mind. Rather, we boarded *Queen Mary 2* for a crossing to New York. This solution offered us the best of both worlds and no compromise. We even ate sushi on the ship!

As my friend Fons will tell you, the answer is never easy; otherwise, everybody would find it. Mediocrity would no longer exist. Wobble boards would balance. Everyone would succeed. The point of Rule 14 is that by seeking 'both' and doing so without the emotional baggage of extremes, we can have better, more generative conversations that move us forward.

My meeting in Copenhagen may have had a difficult start but by reframing it from a compromise-finding mission to an objective assessment of the positives of each position the group managed to move to a reconciliation. They not only agreed but created something new that benefited both teams and, in doing so together, ensured a smooth and fast implementation of the outcome. They didn't settle for mediocrity and average.

You can survive and might even succeed for a time by becoming an expert in compromise. People might thank you for making their lives easier. Success, however, comes from seeing beyond compromise and spotting opportunities. If you want to succeed you will need to be different from the norm. The norm is always in the middle. Success does not lie in the middle. It rests in the top right-hand corner! To move there requires you to understand your biases, as we have seen, but also question your assumptions, as we will now discover with Rule 15.

From rule to lesson

Rule 14 – 'Both' is the only answer to 'either/or' questions

What does Rule 14 teach us? Any organisation is a collection of 'on the one hand, on the other hand' propositions. Whether balancing on the wobble board, or simply managing day-to-day work, organisations are full of dilemmas. Success comes from being able to reconcile these extreme propositions into an innovative solution.

To succeed you will need to remove the emotional biases that lie in the obvious and the entrenched positions. By analysing the positives of both extremes, you can learn to bring them together into a new solution. Being able to gain the positives of one extreme as well as the positives of the other is a positive step. Settling for a bit of each is a retrograde one.

Of course, you can always opt for either or come up with a clever compromise. It will work and it will get you out of an awkward meeting. The higher up you are in an organisation the easier it will be for you to mandate mediocrity, and the blacker and whiter you can become. However, by getting the right people in a room and giving them a process to reconcile 'either-or' you will set the scene for innovation and success to emerge. In a world of shades of grey, the answer to any 'either/or' questions is always 'both'.

Rule 15

'It depends' is the answer to all other questions

Istanbul, Turkey

I'm self-aware enough to know I'll never receive a casting call to play James Bond. Wrong nationality, wrong accent, wrong name, wrong shape. That doesn't mean to say, though, that I've never felt like a secret agent.

The first time was when a CEO laid on a private jet to pick me up at London's Heathrow airport as I arrived on a commercial flight from my monkey conference in Kuala Lumpur to fly me to Spain to speak at his meeting. Hearing someone say 'the plane is ready to go whenever you are, sir' is not something I'd ever experienced before.

The second was flying back from a conference with Dame Stella Rimington DCB, the British author, and former Director General of MI5 with whom I had shared a stage in central Europe. To hear the border agent say to her, in a quiet, deferential voice, 'welcome home ma'am' is not something I had ever witnessed either.

But when it comes to making you feel as though you've stepped into an old-fashioned spy film, nothing beats waking up in Istanbul. Opening the curtains in a room overlooking the misty and mighty Bosphorus to the sounds of the call to prayer is not something you can easily forget. It instantly transports you back to the 1950s.

If you are lucky enough to stay at the Hilton, as I was that morning, the picture is complete. Built at the height of the cold war, the longest-serving Hilton outside the United States is a monument to a bygone era. The walls, adorned with pictures of VIPs who have graced its corridors, hold more secrets than the vast verdant oasis of its grounds could possibly contain.

With all this James Bond day-dreaming, it was almost as if my imagination knew something I didn't, as, unbeknown to me, I was about to learn a lesson about a very special kind of secret.

As I mentioned in our last rule, I am a fan of Istanbul for its beauty, its culture, and, above all, its people. My Turkish acquaintances have always

DOI: 10.4324/9781032639390-18

been generously welcoming, amazingly warm, and always exceedingly good fun. That day was no different.

I was spending time with executives from a tech company. They were shaping their plans and I was there to discuss the implications of these for the organisation.

The company was doing well, so the discussion was going well. The organisation was successful, so the team was successful. I was happy to contribute to storyboarding a growth story rather than helping rewrite one that had led to decline.

The fascinating thing about this team was how long they had been together. So often, fast-paced high-growth organisations, because they are constantly forming and changing, tend to have teams that are also constantly forming and changing. This team, however, was like a family. Its members had grown in stature and status together. Like a family they almost knew what each other was thinking. They could read each other's silences, decode each other's body language, and finish each other's sentences. Only this time, two of them just couldn't understand each other.

The question had been simple. 'What percentage of digital advertising will be watched on mobile devices in ten years' time?' Each had given a very straightforward answer. One had said 20 per cent and the other 70 percent. The fact they disagreed didn't come as a surprise and it wasn't an issue. This team disagreed all the time. That was its strength. What was puzzling was the scale of the disagreement. Never in their collective memory had their answers been so far apart.

But were the answers evidence of an actual disagreement? As we have seen in the last chapter, could the answer be 'both'? That's unlikely. We are not in a dilemma situation. We don't have a 'OOH/OOH' proposition where we must make a choice. What we have here is a demand to make a proposition.

Our executives weren't guessing nor had they been asked to make a number up. They had been asked for their opinion based on their knowledge, experience, and the best data available to them at that point. Given that their knowledge, experience, and data sets were different (after all, what is the point of a team if individuals do not bring any difference to the conversation?) it should not necessarily worry us that the answers were different. But why were they *so* different?

What transpired very quickly was that the discrepancy wasn't in their answers but rather in the assumptions they were making to get to those answers. When asked 'What percentage of digital advertising will be watched on mobile devices in ten years' time?' they defined 'digital advertising' and 'mobile devices' differently. They included different factors in their calculations. Once the differences in definition had been cleared up, the participants agreed on a number.

But would these differences have even come to light if the difference in their answers hadn't been so stark? The answer to this question underpins our ability to succeed. It is only by surfacing, challenging, recording, reviewing, and revising assumptions that we have any chance of continued success.

Assumptions are fundamental to our everyday existence. Given that we have no idea what will happen in the next minute of our lives, we make assumptions. We take certain things to be true not only because we must, but also because we believe them to be probable. On balance, we assume the earth will rotate tomorrow pretty much as it did today, even as our personal world might be turning upside down.

At their simplest, assumptions help us operate. But if we use them to best effect, they can help us succeed.

We have already discussed how competitive advantages are fleeting. We looked at how limiting it is to define ourselves in relation to others. We've tackled the false presumption that to be successful is to win over others. We saw how the only way to be and to remain successful is to learn at a rate higher than the speed of change. This is what assumptions help us do.

When we assume, we state that something is going to happen. In this case we say that either 20 or 70 percent of advertising will be viewed through mobile devices in ten years' time. If the right number ends up being 70 and we planned for 20, or vice versa, we have a problem. Our assumptions were inadequate, and our resulting plans flawed. That's not much of a success.

Arguably, by having more people discuss assumptions we have more of a chance to get them right. But what if everyone in the room had the same wrong thought? After all, groupthink is a real issue in any team. This is the very reason why assumptions need to be revised on an ongoing basis. Reviewing assumptions continually is about asking 'what do I know now that I did not know when I made the assumption?' or 'do I know anything now that is pertinent to the assumption I made previously?'. These questions are learning questions. They generate new insights which in turn generate new plans.

In terms of our Turkish team's success, therefore, the problem was neither their answers, nor their assumptions, nor the difference between these. The problem was the fact that their assumptions had remained secret.

It is by remaining secret (kept or meant to be kept unknown or unseen by others) that an assumption (something accepted as true or as certain to happen) becomes a guess (an estimate or conclusion formed without sufficient information to be sure of being correct). Assumptions that stay secret cannot be checked. They cannot be revised. They cannot generate any insights.

As the definition of secret suggests, there are two reasons why things remain unknown. One is omission and the other deception.

Deception is rare. In my experience people seldom hide their assumptions from others (at least when these people are in the same team or organisation). People may accentuate some assumptions and downplay others in the process of influencing someone. We have all seen business plans with two outrageous extreme propositions that aim to push the decision maker to a desired outcome in the middle. But in the main most assumptions are secret out of omission.

There are instances where people may be reluctant to state their assumptions for fear that any mistake may have consequences (if applied well, our 'See and be seen' rule makes this a non-issue).

Much more frequent is people omitting to state their assumptions either because they are not aware of making them, or because they dismiss them as pathways to decision making (a bit like when you showed only the answer to a maths problem at school and not your workings, believing the answer was more important to your teacher).

The more expert we become at anything, the more we forget the assumptions we make. This is why parents are so bad at teaching their children to drive. We can't teach because we can't break what we know into chunks of assumptions; we have become unconsciously competent. Our children can't learn because 'it is like this because it is' does not explain anything.

What is obvious to us is only so because of assumptions we never disclose, either because we are so used to them that we no longer even realise we have them, or because we simply assume everyone else has them too.

This is the reason why we all need to become spies, able to unearth secrets that lie dormant within us, our teams, and our organisations. I found the best way to do this on that day in Istanbul. I proposed a rule for the rest of workshop which the team then adopted in their modus operandi and which I include here as Rule 15. This rule is that when faced with any question asking for a response rather than a choice, the only possible answer is 'it depends'.

'What percentage of digital advertising will be watched on mobile devices in ten years' time?' It depends! It depends on what? Well, it depends on how you define the terms in the question. It depends on your assumptions for the trajectory in advertising budgets. It depends on your assumptions on the rate of tech replacement in households. And so on. 'It depends' is your main tool as a spy. 'It depends' forces expansion rather than conclusion.

By answering with 'it depends', we surface the unspoken assumptions, so we are able then to record, monitor, and review them, and in turn learn and succeed. Without 'it depends' we are leaving too much to chance. The paradox for leaders, though, is that regardless of whether you answer 'both' or 'it depends', you still have to choose a course of action. This is why we have our next, and final, rule of the 'how' section.

From rule to lesson

Rule 15 – 'It depends' is the answer to all other questions

Any decision we make rests on a set of assumptions. It is only by surfacing these assumptions that we can learn. It is only by monitoring them that we can adjust our plans. It is only by revising plans that turn out to be based on false assumptions that we can succeed.

The problem is that most assumptions are unspoken. Whether it is because we are no longer even aware that we are making them, or because we assume that everybody else is making the same ones, we seldom share them.

To succeed we need to ask what underpins our decisions and bring to the fore the conflicting assumptions that lie dormant in our teams. By answering every question with 'it depends' we ensure that we explore the definitions of the terms contained in the questions as well as the assumptions made in our answers. Doing so will guarantee that we have made richer decisions as well as avoided misunderstandings that could derail implementation.

Rule 16

Leading is choosing

Melbourne, Australia

I've never understood why some things stick in our brains for much longer than others. There are so many events, so many pictures, so many sounds we hear in our childhood. Why do some stay in our minds and others disappear?

I can still hear his voice. I can recall his face. I can see his demeanour, but I couldn't remember his name. I had to check with my sister so that I could write about Monsieur Benard. He was my history teacher when I was about 12 years old.

I don't remember many of the facts and figures Mr Benard taught us, but I do remember him taking us to the archaeological digs he directed in the town of Alise-Sainte-Reine, one of Julius Caesar's key conquests during the Gallic wars. I remember the excitement I felt coming across the remains of a wall I took to be part of a palace. I can also still feel the utter disappointment I felt at being told I had, in fact, uncovered a Roman public toilet!

There is also a phrase Mr Benard used and an attitude he instilled in his young pupils that is forever seared on my brain. 'There is always a choice', he used to say, 'so when you say that you don't have a choice, what you actually mean is that you are not prepared to pay the price associated with the choice you know you should make.'

I've never understood why a 12-year-old brain would have chosen to file away this piece of advice over any other. I have thought it a wise rule on quite a few occasions and, on many, a yardstick against which to measure leadership. It came back to me again one day in Melbourne when I witnessed someone paying a heavy price for having the courage to make a choice that so many, so often, fail to make.

This was our last evening in Australia. Katherine and I were having dinner in the business district of the city having just delivered a workshop it had taken months to design. It had gone well so we decided to treat

DOI: 10.4324/9781032639390-19

ourselves, at our own expense (in case our Australian client is reading these lines), prior to our long journey home.

The table next to ours was occupied by six men celebrating the closure of what must have been a pretty good deal judging by the number of dishes being brought to the table and the number of empty bottles on it. We didn't know what business they were in or which organisation they worked for. We weren't trying to listen in, but they were loud. It was difficult to ignore their conversation.

Having replayed, at length, every minute of the meeting they had just attended, they started to talk about the various, and seemingly numerous, dysfunctions of their organisation. Eventually the latest appointments were discussed and one of the men made a comment. 'Come on guys, we all know it. We know why she got the job. You know they've been desperate to get a woman on the exec team for years.'

I'd love to say it was the unusual nature of this statement that made us look back. But it is still, unfortunately, such a commonly uttered sentiment when male colleagues get together that it was hardly surprising. What made it, however, unusual enough for Katherine and me to turn around was what happened next.

While his colleagues nodded and smirked, one of the men stood up and rather loudly said, 'That is so crass. It's so unacceptable. I can't believe you guys are still talking this kind of *nonsense* [actually he used an expletive that my editor would reject]. She got the job because, quite frankly, she is head and shoulders above all of us and no amount of *sexism* [another expletive was used] is going to explain your failure to get the promotion. She'll be great in the new job. You know it and I know it. Even if you can't accept it. I'm done here. I'll pay my share of the bill on the way out.'

It is deplorable that someone standing up to sexism is so rare as to be noteworthy. But when the price of this choice is exclusion from a group, few human beings have the strength to pay it. That's why most people choose to do nothing. Many are so small-minded as to agree, a few so weak that they feel the need to collude, but most are just unwilling to pay the price of doing what's right. A person's need to belong is often stronger than their need to be right or just. No wonder Mr Benard's Romans used banishment from the city as an alternative to the death penalty.

The Melbourne story is a story of leadership. It is a story about choosing what is right over what is popular or expedient. It is a story which shows that choosing to do nothing is choosing to *be* nothing. It also shows us the mechanics of decision making. It reveals that there are two variables that determine whether a decision is easy or hard to make.

The first is our ability to determine what the right choice is. In this case it is not that hard to know that standing up to sexism is right. The second is our ability to identify the price for that choice and our willingness to pay it. In this case, the price that had to be accepted was exclusion from the group. Decision making is about having both the right analysis and the core strength to make the right choice. Let's tackle both in turn.

When it comes to having the right analysis, the difficulty will increase depending on the focus of the decision.

Some decisions will have to be made about what you do. In Melbourne these were the decisions our business people had made to prepare whatever deal they had just closed. What price were they going to set for whatever they were selling? Who were they going to involve in the pitch? Who would they mobilise to deliver the product/project?

The challenge with these 'what to do' decisions is to ensure the team is competent enough to make the analysis and is given enough autonomy to do so. Otherwise, every decision will need to be escalated and this leads to decision-making being suboptimal and slow. The key for success is to focus on capability (are we equipped to analyse), standards (is everyone clear about what success looks like), and authority (is the right person empowered to make the decision). This is important because, by design, only difficult decisions should reach leaders. If you find yourself taking numerous easy 'what' decisions, you either lack capability around you or the ability to delegate to others.

As well as decisions to be made on 'what we do', we are also called to make choices regarding 'how we do things'. These 'how' decisions are mostly about building capability in the organisation. Do we have the right people, the right processes, the right culture, and the right focus?

'How do we eradicate sexism from our culture?' is a 'how' decision that our fellow diners' organisation would do well to tackle. 'How do I role-model the behaviours we need to get the culture we seek?' is a decision that only one of them felt equipped to take.

The analysis for 'how' decisions is more complex than that needed for 'what' choices. Given that we are focused on reimagining our organisation, the possibilities are endless. Success lies beyond what we already do and know. The key to an effective analysis is to have sufficient relationships inside and outside the organisation to determine all the possibilities open to us.

It is impossible to change 'what we have' without some insights into 'what we could have'. To surface options, you will need to show interest beyond your role. You will need to be as curious about what happens beyond your market as you are familiar with what goes on in it.

Having conducted the analysis to make the right choice we now need to consider the price element of decision making. What are its variables?

The price of any decision can be quantified in hard and soft currency. The hard currency will usually be expressed in terms of money, time, quality, and resources needed for the path chosen. How much, how long, how well, and by whom are questions we need to answer in order to decide. The soft currency is determined by the consequences of failure. What will it cost to make the wrong call, in terms of pay, prospects, promotions, popularity, etc.?

When it comes to the price to pay for choosing, we must ensure we, and those around us, are confident in our ability to cope with the hard and soft costs associated with the right option. Otherwise, we will forever settle on a suboptimal one. There are a number of options open to us to ensure others feel rich enough to be able to pay the price for their decisions.

First, we must specify the hard budget at their disposal. Part of setting standards is to be clear about the costs the organisation is prepared to pay as well as the amount it is prepared to lose. If people do not understand what they can risk, they will either not take any risks at all, or risk it all.

Second, we must offer reassurance regarding the soft price of a decision. We must role-model the behaviours we want to see. We must bear the costs ourselves when the right decisions of others turn out to be the wrong choices. Conversely, we must openly challenge the wrong choices being made for expediency or ease.

When it comes to our own ability to pay for our choices, we must remember that the price of such decisions will invariably involve the cost of potential ostracisation we witnessed in Melbourne. When we make choices, even if these don't change the people involved themselves, they will still change the way these people need to work and behave.

In my experience any decision that has an impact on the human element of the organisation carries a price few leaders are prepared to pay. Many would rather do nothing than risk paying too much.

It is therefore important to remember that your role is not to make people happy but to make them stronger and more capable. Leading is about choosing being right over being comfortable; it is to serve rather than be popular. In this way, decision making is not just about choosing a course of action but about the intentionality we apply to setting a tone for our organisation. It is about choosing to be remembered for what we stood for rather than what we tolerated.

What our Melbourne dinner taught us is that, when faced with a decision, our rational analysis may well come up with a decision, but it is our emotional resolve that will enable us to enact it. Building personal resilience to enact decisions that others may find unpalatable is about remembering your 'what' of earlier. What is the value you bring if you are not prepared to make tough calls? What discretionary effort will others bring when you can't bring your own? What moral example do you set by not doing what you know is right?

Rule 1 stated that you can succeed. What will change the 'can' into 'will' is your ability to make the right decisions even when the people costs are high. Standing up for what is right is never easy – that's why only one of our six diners did it. It is impossible to stand up for what is right without having the maturity to choose the right path. This path is what the next, and final, section of this book is designed to help you chart. Its four rules are designed to help you uncover the 'why' that lies at the root of executive maturity.

From rule to lesson

Rule 16 – Leading is choosing

Being popular for doing what is popular is following rather than leading. Leading is choosing what is right, irrespective of the personal costs. When it comes to decision making, to succeed we must develop two core competencies.

One is our analytical and conceptual ability. This will enable us to surface the options available to us. The more the decision focuses on how and why we do what we do, the more numerous the choices.

The other competency refers to our ability to bear the costs of making the right choice. The more these costs impact people rather than budgets, the harder they become to make. No one likes being unpopular or ostracised.

Becoming resilient enough to make the right choices requires us to have both a strong moral compass and a strong sense of compassion. The former will stop us from seeking popularity at all costs whilst the latter will protect us from doing what is popular rather than what is right.

Part 3

Why

In 2009 a TED video went viral. So far, so unsurprising.

What set this video apart, however, was how unpolished it appeared compared to the usual output from the much-admired Davos for geeks and hipsters. No red circle for the presenter to stand in. No sharp visuals. No fancy remote. The pre-recorded applause was there, but far too loud and busy for a video that seemed to have been recorded in the back room of a bar.

Shot in a rather tight angle, with a phone-like quality, one young man, sleeves rolled up, standing in front of a flipchart and drawing as he speaks, was taking the invisible audiences through a series of circles. Maybe it was the home-made, amateurish quality of the video that appealed, in the same way a bootleg recording of a concert sparks the imagination. But that wouldn't do justice to this particular TED talk.

I am more of the view that it was the simplicity and the elegance of the model the young man was describing that enthralled the TED audience. Any model is the conceptualisation of a situation. The more complex and multifaceted a situation is, the more clarity and simplicity we crave. The genius of Simon Sinek's TED talk was to make the complex topic of strategy linear and powerfully simple.

Most organisations, he argued, focus on the how and the what. They know what they make and how they make it. As a result, they are limited in their ability to innovate and adapt. They go from the 'what' to the 'how' and end at 'why'. If they travel from the 'why' to the 'how' and the 'what' instead, a multitude of adjacent possibilities open to them.

In many ways, the idea was an extension of what salespeople had been taught decades earlier. Sell benefits, not features – usually explained as 'no one ever buys a drill, what they buy is a hole'. Sinek went one step further by pointing out that actually no one ever buys a hole. They buy a lifestyle – a picture, a new TV, or whatever else that proverbial hole was designed to house.

DOI: 10.4324/9781032639390-20

The talk became a book, Sinek became a management rock star, and the 'search for purpose' became a multimillion-dollar consulting gold mine.

So, why – if the model is so elegant – would I end this book with 'why' rather than start with it? There are two reasons.

The first is that despite valuing simplicity I shy away from simplistic. The model in its elegance omits the interplay between each element thereby limiting the possibilities it seeks to unleash. The relationships between, why, what, and how are far from being linear. The famous Sinek three circles should have never been concentric. Why, what, and how are three parts of a Venn diagram.

Think of your career. Is it a why, a how, or a what that drove it? My guess is all three. As I pointed out in the introduction to the first part of this book, it is likely that you started with the 'what'. You might have informed your 'why' by the 'how' to get there. How much you enjoyed studying, for example, might have led you to make some choices over others. At some stage, you'll have considered the 'why' of that profession's appeal. Whatever you did, you never consciously went through the three in order, nor would you have been able to if you tried.

Finishing with 'why' is no less valuable than starting with it. All we need is to have it somewhere.

But before you accuse me of being a petulant child, acting out of some misplaced jealousy, by doing the opposite of what a much more success-ful author and consultant advises, you should know that I have a second reason for advocating finishing with 'why', in this case.

That reason is recency effect. Our tendency to see recent events as indi-cators of the future (the recency bias) is not a desirable thing, but the fact that we also remember best what we hear last (the recency effect) is advan-tageous to our journey through the rules of success.

Why we do what we do is a complex and uncomfortable domain. It is complex because the changing nature of our values and habits makes them hard to explain. It is uncomfortable because the level of introspec-tion necessary to understand our 'why' forces us to question the essence of the role we have carved out for ourselves. It is easier for us to concentrate on the 'how' and 'what' of success. But while the 'why' may be uncomfort-able, it underpins whether the success you seek will deliver the outcome you crave.

This last part contains the rules that will determine not whether you are successful but whether you will ever be able to judge yourself as such. In a way Sinek shared an important truth: 'why' is an intrinsically more valu-able measure of self-worth, and therefore of a life well lived, than 'what' and 'how' alone. Maybe this simple fact is enough to explain the viral nature of that now iconic video.

Rule 17

Enough > more

Paris, France

I wasn't supposed to be there.

I have had plenty of strange experiences in my life. I have been to some unexpected places. I have witnessed the extremes of human existence. I have sat alongside royalty in the Middle East and walked beside the slums of India and townships of South Africa. I have taken wrong turns in cities to end up on streets I shouldn't have been on and taken left turns on planes to sit in seats I couldn't afford to be in. I have been to places I never even imagined going to as a child. I have been scared, I have been sad, I have been angry, and I have been joyful, but I have never been out of place.

But walking through the doors of the Ritz didn't feel right. I was in Paris, but this was not *my* Paris.

I was born on a housing estate owned by the French railway. My dad was a train driver and my mum a domestic servant. We weren't the poorest in our town, but we certainly weren't the richest. My parents did well and ensured my sister and I did better. They worked hard so we wouldn't have to work harder.

As my paternal grandmother was fond of saying, 'We don't have the best jobs, but this shouldn't stop us from being the best at the jobs we have.' My father retired as a test driver on France's famed high-speed train and my mother took night classes that allowed her to finish her career as a controller for the French tax office. Had they been Americans, they would have been living the American dream.

One of the perks of working on the railway is that you get free travel for your immediate family. My sister and I spent our youth on the tracks. The special trips were when my dad was driving the train. We got to sit right at the front. These were usually our Paris trips. They happened at least once a year and always when we needed clothes.

DOI: 10.4324/9781032639390-21

The shops we went to were a far cry from the designer stores of the Place Vendôme, home of the Ritz. We went to the cut-price clothing retailer, Tati, a French institution located in the mainly west African district of Barbès, at the foot of Montmartre. We loved it. And more than anything we loved watching our dad bargain. He was the best. We never paid the asking price. In any case, given that we didn't have to pay for transport, the clothes ended up cheaper than in our home town and they were, to us, nicer than anything we could have got anywhere in the world.

Our Paris was dirty, smelly, lively, and loud. Place Vendôme is none of these things. It is ordered, clean, quiet, magnificent, and historic. It is beautiful, but it is not *my* Paris. This was not my place and so I felt out of place. I was attending a team-building event a client had asked me to observe. This was not just your typical 'cooking a meal together' event. This event entailed cooking a meal alongside a chef at the world-renowned Escoffier school of the Ritz.

It could have been the words of the chef that I chose to remember: 'The good news is that French butter doesn't make you fat.' Instead, this cooking class brought to mind a conversation I'd had a few years before. This was a conversation I had understood intellectually at the time but now, finally, felt viscerally. It was one that would give rise to this new rule: enough > more.

I had been giving feedback to a CEO who had asked me to work with him and his team. He was incredibly successful by any measure you care to use. He was rich beyond the grasp of most people. He was happily married to someone at the top of their field. He was fêted in his country and surrounded by friends. But it had not always been so.

He described how, when he was still a child, his world had been turned upside down by the unexpected death of his father. His mother had to take on more work to make ends meet. He had to leave the private school his father had scraped his wages together to afford. He tried to help and do his best. He took on jobs of his own and felt responsible for his siblings at an age at which most of us don't even feel accountable for our own actions. He was forever scarred by the experience of the utter poverty fate had left them in. His world had fallen apart in the blink of an eye.

The reason we were discussing his past experiences was to understand his present behaviour. The psychologist Kurt Lewin devised an incredibly elegant model to explain human behaviour. He stated that our behaviour is a function of who we are as a person and the environment we find ourselves in. Often presented as the equation $B=f(P,E)$, Lewin's theory is elegant in its simplicity without being simplistic. It isolates two variables – we as individuals and the situations that we are in – but also recognises that there are many elements that shape who we are and the context we find ourselves in.

By knowing more about the CEO's personal history and the environment he grew up in I was hoping to understand more about his current behaviour and the impact he was having on his business. While he demonstrated high levels of people-focused power, these paled into insignificance in the face of his stratospheric levels of personal performance. He was involved in the minutiae of the business. His team felt he didn't trust them. Above all, they worried that his deep involvement in all things, mixed with an understandable lack of deep expertise in everything, led to suboptimal decisions being taken.

So what was he trying to prove by being everywhere all the time? Why was he finding it so hard to trust others? His answer was simple: 'You never know what happens next and you can't take anything for granted. It could all fall apart in the blink of an eye.'

Lewin's equation was helping me understand how his childhood experiences impacted his adult behaviour. But I was finding it hard to reconcile this with the knowledge I had of my client's current situation. Surely, he had to realise that even if everything went wrong, he would still be just fine. Even if the company collapsed, and he was disgraced, he would still have more than enough to maintain his lifestyle three times over. That's where my Ritz experience helped me make sense of what was going on.

By way of background, I must tell you that I don't do much work in France. I have spent most of my adult life and all of my working life in the UK. As a result, I find it much easier to conduct business in English than in French. Of course, I can still speak French and give a speech in my mother tongue, but I find workshops and long meetings in this language very tiring.

This is the reason why this experience was so different. Despite having been to so many unexpected places I had never felt like a fraud, that is, until I walked through the door of the Ritz and was reminded of past experiences (by my own psyche, I might add, as the staff made me feel incredibly welcome). This is when where I came from, and where I was, collided in a visceral way.

At that stage, I realised that what was standing in the way of my client's success as a leader was the same thing that lay at the heart of my discomfort at the Ritz. Neither of us had defined 'enough' and, as a result, we both were failing to realise that, to succeed, 'enough' is superior to 'more'. Let me explain.

We are all the products of a drive for more. Whether it is more control (as was the case for my client), more comfort (as was mine at the Ritz), more security, more relationships, more space, or more freedom, there is always a 'more' at the root of our desires. Yet, although this search for more gives us the momentum to succeed, left unmanaged, it carries the seeds for our downfall.

The problem is that we are looking for more in the rear-view mirror. When we want more, what we are saying is that we no longer want what we had. This search for 'more' becomes an end in itself. It can never be satisfied. We become dysfunctional as we can't possibly assess either of Lewin's variables (person and environment). We are so busy looking back that we can't see our present behaviour or how it impacts our current situation.

The key to our success lies in our ability to drive looking ahead rather than looking back. We need to act out of consideration and determination rather than instinct and happenstance. We need to proactively shape our environment rather than react to our circumstances. We can only do this if we understand 'enough'. Only by defining what is enough can we stop wanting more and, instead, focus on wanting better.

Whether we call it maturity, or, for the more psychologically minded, the avoidance of hedonistic adaptation (i.e., stopping taking what we have for granted in the pursuit of what we don't have), we succeed when we understand that we are enough, as well as when we have enough.

Maturity is not about knowing everything. It is about knowing ourselves. It is about understanding how to play to our strengths and mitigate our flaws. It is about being comfortable enough in our own skin to stop having to prove ourselves, preferring instead to improve ourselves. It is about being dissatisfied with the world *and* being grateful to be in a position to change it. It is about being audacious in our goals *but* humble in our assessment of our own capability to achieve them.

Executive maturity, at its simplest and most critical, is about managing our own emotions and relationships with others so that the choices we make are informed by the situations we are in, rather than the emotions we experience. Executive maturity does not come with age but with the mastery of three abilities.

The first is the ability to define our 'enough'. Without knowing what is enough, getting more has no value. Rule 1 made us define both our objectives and why they mattered. This rule demands that we go back to this definition and refine it.

Let's assume my client's Rule 1 definition of success was 'I want to be at the top of my organisation to impact positively the lives of others so that I can achieve financial independence'. We have the 'what' (i.e., being at the top of the organisation, impacting positively the lives of others) and the 'why' (i.e., achieving financial independence). We are missing the 'enough'.

It's ok to never be satisfied by 'good enough' but we need to remember that the opposite of 'good enough' is not 'more', it is 'better'. Only by knowing what enough impact and financial security looks like will my client be able to focus on the reality of his current situation rather than past desires and future dreams. Without defining 'enough', my client, just like a teenager in search of a dopamine hit, will act to satisfy a craving rather than planning a route for success.

The second ability we need in order to develop executive maturity is the ability to recognise our emotional triggers. The good news for us is that while human beings are pretty difficult to understand, they are relatively easy to predict. We tend to behave in similar ways when faced with similar circumstances. Our problem is that we don't always recognise this ourselves.

In our personal lives we rely on trusted others to warn us when we are about to do, yet again, that thing we promised ourselves we'd never do again. Others recognise the triggers. The same should be true for leaders. Relying on colleagues and followers for advice with our own emotional monitoring increases both their levels of trust in us and their engagement.

By being more open to our need for support we become more transparent and therefore easier to follow. There is also an added benefit to enlisting others to help with emotional regulation. Displaying our own vulnerability not only increases our own maturity but generates a climate of openness in the organisation. It ensures that issues are surfaced earlier, and options shared sooner. It's this that leads to the third ability required to master maturity.

This is our ability to develop gratefulness. Being grateful is not about being nice or deluded. There is a lot to be angry and disappointed about in the world, in others, and in ourselves as individuals. The problem is one of balance. Being grateful is about restoring balance to the way we assess both ourselves and the situations we are in.

The search for more comes from a deficit view of the world and our place in it. When we want more, we want to fill a gap. By our having a flawed assessment of people and situations the gap becomes a chasm and the chasm a bottomless pit which can never be filled. No amount of effort will ever make us or the environment better.

By being grateful we are forced to see what is in and around us. Being grateful helps us gauge what more is needed in order to ensure that we have enough. Being grateful brings us back to the reality of the environment we find ourselves in, enabling us to adopt the appropriate behaviour to shape it for the better. It is only when we understand what 'enough' looks like that we can decide how to tackle Lewin's equation – which our next rule tells us we must do.

From rule to lesson

Rule 17 – Enough > more

Our first rule asked us to define success. What did we want to achieve and why did it matter to us to achieve this? Invariably, our definition will be rooted in the desire for more of something. Whether psychological or physical, whether future-focused or intended as a way to preserve the present or return to the past, our success criteria articulate a desire to avoid, prevent, or alleviate dissatisfaction.

This legitimate need for more can quickly become a recipe for less. Being focused on wanting 'more' can only be of value if we define what 'enough' looks like. Without 'enough' our attention is locked on our need for more rather than focused on wanting something better.

Executive maturity, the objective assessment of why we do what we do so as to manage our emotions proactively rather than react instinctively, is the only way we can stay on the path to success. We achieve this by mastering three capabilities.

First, we need to be capable of refining our definition of success so that it is underpinned by a genuine understanding of what enough looks like. Second, we need to build a network of trusted collaborators who can help us recognise the triggers that hijack our emotions, so we act in accordance with our desires even under pressure. Third, we have to develop a mindset of gratitude which forces us to assess objectively our reality.

Hired, mired, fired

Milan, Italy

For decades, organisational psychologists have tried to understand why two people can be the same on paper yet so different in real life. Take the following two individuals.

They both belong to what in French we call 'the third age' or what the more subtle English would describe as 'of a certain age'. They are both British and knighted (although while the late Queen herself performed the ceremony for one she is said to have refused doing so for the other). They are both at the top of their profession. They are both globally famous icons. They are incredibly rich. They possess more homes, throughout Britain and abroad, than they could possibly ever need. So far, this is not commonplace but not unheard of either.

They are both divorced. Their first wives have graced the covers of magazines. Editors the world over paid thousands of dollars for pictures of both women. They have children, some who live in England and some abroad. They also both have five grandchildren each. They are even rumoured to have dated the same aristocratic woman in their youth. They both head royal families, one literally, one figuratively. Now it's starting to be more unusual.

I am, of course, talking about King Charles III, head of the British monarchy, and Sir Mick Jagger, king of rock and roll and lead singer of The Rolling Stones. These are two people who may well look similar on paper, but I hazard a guess that an evening with either would feel rather different. This was the thought in my mind as I left my second meeting of the day in Milan.

I was in Italy for a few days of work and had managed to arrange a couple of early catch-up meetings with two leaders I had worked with in the past. They were as similar on paper but as different in person as the two above.

Both were British but lived in Milan. One worked in the FMCG sector, the other in financial services. Both headed their respective businesses.

DOI: 10.4324/9781032639390-22

They were both in their early forties, married with two children. They both had homes in the UK and abroad. Their financial situation might not have been comparable to that of our two kings, but they were doing very well. They were also, as far as one can tell when looking only through the lens of friendship, happy.

They even shared a passion for flying (as seems to be the case with many well-off, middle-aged men). One flew his own helicopter and the other a leased plane. I might add that the one flying the helicopter had built it himself, which demanded progressively more creativity on my part to find ways to decline the regular invitations to 'come for a ride'. Above all, at least for our purpose, they were both highly regarded, successful, and in demand. They also had both just changed jobs.

Let's start with the helicopter pilot. He is what I would call a turn-around specialist. He takes a failing business and transforms it, in record time, into a high-performing one. He is a passionate 'fixer' which might explain the helicopter. He gets under the skin of a business, gives people clarity, sets standards, develops his team, and gets results. I first met him when he was leading an operation in Germany. He was halfway through the transformation of the business. I hadn't seen him since then.

As we sat down for a coffee, I asked him to bring me up to date. 'The turnaround was going to plan and then they fired me,' he said, before letting out one of the loud guffaws his employees valued as much as his leadership skills. I must have looked puzzled, wondering how he could have been fired given that he still worked for the same organisation, so he explained. 'What I mean is that I had done what I could do and what they needed me to do. We all knew that if I'd carried on, I would have turned the business around again. It was time for me to move me on. No one wants a turned-around business to turn around again. I was at risk of transforming the operation into a fan!'

He hadn't been fired, but he had been moved on. In fact, he had been moved on for the very same reasons he had been hired in the first place. He was now turning around another failing operation in another country until, I guess, the rotors of his helicopter would need to turn again, at some point, to minimise the risk of him turning this new business around again.

Having caught up with the king of turnaround it was time for me to see the king of high performance. I met our aeroplane pilot banker in his office. He too was in a new city. He had moved to Milan with his family, a year earlier, after accepting the top job in a financial services firm. Unlike my first interlocutor, his role was not about transforming failing businesses into high-performing ones but taking high-performing businesses to the next level. As he was fond of explaining to me when we first met, the journeys from bad to good and good to great are relatively straightforward. The challenge is to take a great business and make it greater.

He has one of the most strategic minds I have come across. That's why he had been recruited to his previous company. He was both conceptual and analytical which, in my experience, is a rare combination. His career had been as nomadic as that of the helicopter pilot. We first met in London where he moved from project to project as and when the business needed to break new ground. But, unlike my first interlocutor, he now no longer worked for the same employer. 'You could say I was fired' was the first thing he said when I asked him why.

It occurred to me, as I was preparing this book, that this story may not cast me in the best light. Two successful executives, both working with Emmanuel, and both end up being fired! It is often said that no one ever gets fired for hiring the McKinsey consulting company – had I become the flipside of McKinsey? Anyway, I decided to cast my pride aside for the sake of this chapter. To be fair, he hadn't really been fired, in the sense of having done something wrong that led to his dismissal.

He had closed another successful project and was about to be moved again when he decided he wanted to do something different. He felt ready to take on more responsibilities and lead an established business over time. His employer however was keen to keep him where he was, not convinced he would be as successful in the new place in which he wanted to be. Faced with a stalemate, he had chosen to move on. In fact, he made this choice for the very same reason he had been hired in the first place – his need to go from great to greater.

So here we are with two stories of people 'fired' and both for the same reasons they were hired. I chose these two because of their symmetry and also because of their differences. I could have chosen others. This type of story is the norm in most workplaces. You will have met the people who were recruited because they were different and who then got fired because they 'didn't fit'. You will know the 'much-needed' rule breakers who were eventually removed for breaking one rule too many, the mavericks whose non-conformity led to their downfall, and the steady hands who were eventually judged not impulsive enough.

It is a common story that replays itself ad infinitum for a very simple reason. Organisations recruit for something they haven't got, yet, being built for predictability, they value what they have. The firing does not occur because of the wrong hiring but because people get stuck. Either people become stuck in a role or a rut. I chose these two stories because, unlike countless others I have witnessed, the two executives took their destiny in their own hands.

The helicopter pilot was stuck in a role he loved which the organisation valued. That's a good place to be stuck in. He was happy. The organisation was happy. He made sure he moved from project to project before the rot set in. The aeroplane pilot, on the other hand, was stuck in a role he no longer wanted. The organisation had put him in a box he no longer wanted to be in. Unable to persuade his bosses of his potential, he had to move in order to become who he wanted to be.

Lewin, who we met in our last rule, was right. There are only two variables open to us to get out of the mire we are stuck in. Remember his equation B=f(P,E). In our first story we found an executive who had to change the situation in order to continue to be the person he is. In the second, our executive had to change his situation to be the person he wanted to be.

This rule demands that you understand where the junction is and which path to take to reach the destination you have specified for yourself. There is always a junction; the only question is who chooses the path. Will you be able to change the situation before the organisation decides to change you as a person?

To know which of 'person' or 'situation' to address we first need to understand your goal. In Lewis Carroll's *Alice's Adventures in Wonderland*, Alice finds herself at a crossroads. Desperate to know which way to go, she asks the Cheshire Cat for some help. He asks her for her destination. Upon hearing that she does not have one in mind, he tells her, 'Then it doesn't much matter which way you go.' If you don't know where you are going, all roads lead there!

I will assume – given we have already covered this topic in Rule 1 (You can succeed) and refined it in our last rule (Enough > more) – that, unlike Alice, you do know where you want to go. It is worth remembering, though, that often our goals will change as our experience grows. We may have had detours along the way that cause us to question our overall direction. It is important therefore to recognise the need to continuously review our goals. But let's assume you know where you want to go.

We can then work the rule in the order it is stated – start with 'hired', understand 'mired', and avoid 'fired'.

Do you know why you were hired? It may seem like a silly question, but it is actually quite a difficult one to answer. Sure, you were hired to fill a gap. The organisation needed someone to do something. That's the easy part. The more difficult one is why did they need you? What is it in you that they valued over and above what they could have got with someone else? It is a difficult question because the answers to it are often unstated (at least beyond skills and knowledge).

It is critical to spend time researching and understanding what the organisation sees in you. Our third rule (EST and ER do not spell value) should help you identify what the organisation values in you. Whatever these attributes are, they are as much the seeds of your downfall as the sources of your success. Leaders in the organisation will not only want you to behave in line with their expectations but will assume that this is the only value you can bring. This was the issue for my airline pilot. He was so good at showing them what they wanted to see that they did not expect to see anything else.

It is only when you understand the goal you have, and the value they see, that you can identify why you might become mired. Only then will you be able to decide which variable of the equation you need to work on so as not to get stuck. There are three scenarios.

If the value others see is in line with the goals you have, you don't have an issue. Your main task is to ensure your performance is in line with their expectations. You may need to move to another project (as was the case in our first story) but you won't have to change. The only note of caution is to ensure you continue to be challenged. Comfort can quickly lead to boredom and boredom leads to, at best, average. Organisations seldom reward average performance.

The second scenario is that you are stuck because the value they see is not on a par with the goals you have. Your organisation is comfortable with who you are and unable to see who you want to be. This was the case in our second story. This is the point at which you have to decide whether you are going to work on the person (i.e., you) or the situation (i.e., the role). It is the curse of high performance that the better you do in a role the more people will want to keep you there. Its gift is that high performance gives you opportunities to move on. Moving on is not the only option, though.

Part of the issue many people have in this situation is that they reinforce the views of their leaders. They think that they only need to do even more in their current role to be identified as candidates for opportunities outside this. This is a flawed assumption. Success comes from understanding that you need to do what is best in your current role and, as well as this, do something different.

You need to act as who you are, plus the person you want to become, rather than simply the person others want you to be. You need to excel in your current role and display the skills of the one you want. Then you will stand a chance of being as credible a candidate for this in their eyes as you are in your own.

The third, and all too common, scenario is that you get stuck as a caricature of the person you thought you needed to be. You become blind to who you could be and, sadly, who you thought you could become. This is the most difficult and challenging situation to be in – it is what I call a double-sided sticky tape situation. The organisation has stuck you in a role and you keep providing more glue.

The only way you can see something you are blind to is by ensuring other people act as your eyes. High-performing individuals in fields from business to sport have coaches. These people give them ways to assess their performance honestly. You don't have to pay to have one. Coaches are all around you. From your friends to your colleagues, peers, and mentors, find a network where you are comfortable to explore what is possible outside what you see.

The rule is clear – you will eventually be fired for the reasons you were hired. Whether it is your decision or not depends on the work you do to develop the self-awareness to proactively shape your destiny. Our next rule will help.

From rule to lesson

Rule 18 – Hired, mired, fired

You have met them all. You have seen people being hired for the very attributes that would eventually cause their downfall. They're the rule-breakers, the rain-makers, the analysts, and the catalysts, all recruited for their differences by organisations that value conformity most of all. Being fired, however, is not an inevitability.

The lesson that comes from this rule is simple: don't become a caricature and get stuck in a role that doesn't fulfil your goal.

To navigate the inevitable inflection point you will need to be clear about both your goal and the value the organisation sees in you. Knowing both, you can focus on assessing how aligned they are. You will need to do so regularly as your career and goals evolve. If there is a gap, the solution is not to do more of the same but rather to do more of something else alongside delivering your current accountabilities. Deliver on your current role but behave as though you already have the next one.

Rule 19

You are dispensable

Nant Gwrtheyrn, Wales

I don't know what it is about me, cliffs, and cars. We just don't seem to get along.

The first time I realised this was in Monaco. I could have sworn the taxi driver taking me from Nice airport to my hotel in Monte Carlo, where I was due to speak the following day, thought he was training for the Grand Prix. The speed at which he was taking the bends on the narrow road up the mountain was breathtakingly fast. The cliffs never looked so frightening. The Mediterranean at the bottom never appeared so forbidding.

The second time it happened to me was in India. The heavy rains of the monsoon had shut down the main road taking us to the remote hillside venue where I was due to co-facilitate a week-long workshop. Unperturbed, my taxi driver decided that the fields along the mountainside would serve just as well as a road. I wasn't sure whether to keep my seatbelt on in the event of an accident or undo it in case I needed to jump should he take us over the cliff. The thundering torrent at the bottom of the ravine was deafening.

This time, though, in Wales, I was driving so had only myself to blame. I was just praying no one was coming the other way. Driving from London to north Wales is never straightforward. Trying to get from one to the other, via the Eryri National Park, in an electric car is an adventure. Doing so in the dark is not easy. But coming down a cliff edge on a single-track road, with a gradient of 1 in 4 and two hairpin corners, is just plain scary. The Irish Sea looked bleak.

Let me put your mind at rest. I am not about to embark on some sort of analogy between your career and falling off a cliff! I am merely mentioning the landscape because, unlike our previous rules that have been inspired by people or events, this one was influenced by a place.

I was coming down that hill (not that going up it is any easier) to speak at an annual event for senior civil servants working in Wales. This event meant a lot to me. Being invited to attend was an honour, but also

DOI: 10.4324/9781032639390-23

nerve-wracking, and not just because of the hill. I left France in 1985 having won a scholarship to attend an international sixth form college located in Wales. I owe so much to Wales that having the opportunity to give back to the country that shaped me was a privilege I didn't take lightly.

The venue for the event was the village of Nant Gwrtheyrn (don't worry, I can't pronounce it either and, unlike you, I have no excuse). It is named after the valley where it is located. It lies in isolation by the sea at the foot of Yr Eifl (that's ər ˈəivl phonetically). A former quarrying village abandoned midway through World War II, it is now a Welsh Language and Heritage Centre.

Thankfully the road, known locally as 'Screw Hill', has been renovated. Carved out of the rock to access the village, it was originally an unpaved single-track road with unprotected edges, no passing places, six hairpin corners, and a gradient making it totally unsuitable for ordinary cars and impassable in the treacherous weather Wales is known for. Coming down was considered so difficult that it was frequently used as a sporting challenge and the pioneering news service, British Pathé, described driving back up as 'Climbing the Unclimbable'.

Despite so much research and so many advances, we still know so little about how our brains function. Yet, I am pretty sure that it wouldn't take an fMRI scanner to see the connections that led mine to think, as I parked in front of the main hall, 'what would they have done if I hadn't made it?' There does seem to be a certain inevitability, in my experience at least, that once the danger has passed, thoughts of survival turn to thoughts about mortality.

I met most of the team members who had invited me to speak at this event some 15 years ago. While I know that, especially in the civil service, business and friendship should not mix, I would like to think that they would have missed me. I am in no doubt that, professionally at least, my absence would have caused some issues. Crashing down that hill would have messed up the flow of the week! But the truth is that once the shock had passed, even if this particular event might have been disrupted or cut short, their work would have continued.

As my father always taught me (although it turns out that General Charles de Gaulle had said it before him), 'The cemeteries of the world are full of indispensable men.' What this rule is about is seeing this thought for what it is. Rather than a sad, morbid, or even debilitating thought, leaders need to think about the idea of being dispensable as being freeing.

The fact that someone will eventually take our place does not free us from the consequences of our actions but should free us from the fear of taking these actions. The fact that whatever we do will eventually be built upon or undone by someone else should free us from the fear of laying a foundation stone.

Our being dispensable and, in the end, easily replaceable puts an emphasis on our contribution. We will not be judged by our longevity, or our custody of the past, but by our contribution to the future. What the view from the hill taught me is that there are two ways to approach success. One is to be the best in the environment we are in, the other is to do our best to change the environment we inhabit.

That's the Nant Gwrtheyrn rule: You are dispensable, but you can be remembered for the marks you left on the landscape.

Even when you find yourself in a start-up situation, there is always an existing landscape. No one ever leads from a blank sheet. Even if there is no company to lead, the people you will bring together have history. There is always a past to contend with. What the Welsh Language and Heritage Centre of Naant Gwrtheyrn highlights are the three possibilities open to us as leaders. We can ignore the past, we can build on the past, or we can use it to springboard to the future.

The people who forget about the past are often the people who don't know why they are leading. They are those unlikely to succeed. You cannot lead unless you want to change something, and you cannot change anything unless you are aware of what is already there and why it is there. Even if you want to introduce something new, to do something that has never been done, you have to be cognisant of what has gone on before. You have to learn from the past. You cannot be a leader, never mind a successful one, by ignoring the past.

Many leaders, however, get so caught up in the past that they are frozen by it. They see their role as custodians of it. They try to maintain the trajectory. They make some incremental adjustments. They learn so much from the past that they don't think they have anything to teach the future. They do what has been done. They try to do it better, maybe a little differently. They build on it. You can be a leader, and a good one at that, by building on the past. But you cannot be a truly successful one, in the same way you cannot be a successful silversmith if all you do is polish other people's artefacts.

There is another way to think about leadership, though. It is the way successful leaders think. They use their knowledge of the past not to build on it, but to kickstart the future. I call this mindset being a steward rather than a custodian.

With etymological roots in the words 'house' and 'guardian', stewardship originally referred to the duties of household servants but later came to describe the acceptance of responsibility for not only safeguarding, but also shepherding the valuables of others.

It is described in the international standard ISO 20121 as the 'responsibility for sustainable development shared by all those whose actions affect environmental performance, economic activity, and social progress, reflected as both a value and a practice by individuals, organisations, communities, and competent authorities.'

I define being a steward simply as taking the responsibility to guide and develop a company in the service of sustainable, continued development. Understanding that we are dispensable helps us see our position on a continuum from what has gone on before to what will happen next. Being a steward is knowing that our role is not just to understand the past and ensure we have a future, but also to show the willingness and wherewithal to take us there.

This stewardship mindset is about hope. This is why compassion is more important than empathy. Hope is about knowing where we are in order to highlight a future desired state (goal) that can be reached (will) through a series of steps (way). That hope rests on an acknowledgement of what has gone on before, but it cannot exist without a will to build a future. That's the rule. If you don't have an insatiable desire to build the future, you have no right to lead. To succeed you have to understand the past and speak to the future.

To be steward you need to be clear about 'why tomorrow will be better than today'. To have a steward mindset you have to have a vision. It doesn't have to be a grand plan or a revolutionary vision, it just has to be something that drives you forward and drives others towards you. 'I want the financial rewards that come with success' may be your reason to want to lead, but it's hardly going to be a good enough vision for others to want to follow.

Knowing what marks you want to make on the landscape is necessary, but not sufficient, for success. Stewards must have the will to make the marks and the way to make them if they stand any chance of taking people on the journey. They must, as we have said previously, display strong people-focused power.

Let's get back to Nant Gwrtheyrn. The quarry produced setts; ironically, given the state of the route down the hill, these are the stone blocks used for road surfacing. With products shipped out and goods arriving in, by the Irish sea, the community was isolated. When the quarry closed, the community dispersed. The only visible signs of existence left were the scars on the landscape, the ruins of quarry buildings, and the workers' cottages being reclaimed by nature.

There were many plans for the redevelopment of the site. Eventually it was acquired by a trust set up by Carl Clowes, a medical doctor brought up in England by his Welsh mother and English father who eventually settled in Wales.

His idea in founding the Nant Gwrtheyrn Trust was to buy the village, to restore and regenerate it, to set up a Welsh language centre. As a steward, he chose to use the foundations of the past to shape the future. He chose to honour the people who had left by inviting new people to come. He created a language and heritage centre so that their stories could continue to be told in the language in which they were lived. That was the mark he wanted to leave on this already scarred landscape.

Dr Clowes could have chosen to create an industrial museum on the grounds. He could have just maintained what was already there. He could have polished the buildings where people once polished the stone. He could have been a caretaker. Instead, he chose to be a steward.

Stewardship is not the same as day-dreaming though. He didn't just need a knowledge of the past and a vision of the future. He needed to make it happen. He had to get enough people to spend enough money so that enough of us would drive down that hill to shape a different future for all of us.

What about us? When others are called to put the letters RIP after our names, what will we be called? Will we have been caretaker or steward? Both are worthy professions. Both are necessary occupations. But only by being the latter will we have led. Only stewards can answer the question 'why did you lead?'. Dr Crowes answered it with gusto.

I slept well that night after the eventful drive. Not too soundly – I did after all have a literal hill to climb the following day – but I knew that whether or not I made it, I was dispensable enough that I could safely go and state my truth at the event.

I knew that to succeed, I just had to leave a mark on the future the participants were trying to shape for a country I care deeply about. I knew I would have to work hard to succeed and, in the end, our last rule would help me should I fail.

From rule to lesson

Rule 19 – You are dispensable

'We are all replaceable' seems like a good summary of Rule 18. So what? That's hardly a revelation, never mind a lesson. The fact that the world hasn't stood still despite, to the best of demographers' estimates, one hundred and nine billion fellow human beings having died since the dawn of our species, makes that point rather adequately. There is no doubt that, even when our own existence ends, life does go on.

Where Rule 3 helped us define the value we can add, this nineteenth rule forces us to ask why we want to add it. We know we can lead but why do we want to? The lesson is that our being dispensable is a freeing and enabling thought, rather than a morbid one.

While it does not free us from the consequences of our actions, the fact that someone will eventually take our place, should free us from the fear of taking them. The fact that whatever we do will eventually be built upon or undone by someone else, enables us to lay a foundation stone.

That we are dispensable and, in the end, replaceable, puts an emphasis on our contribution. We will not be judged by our longevity, or our custody of the past, but by our contribution to the future.

The lesson is simple. Will you be a caretaker, or will you be a steward? Will you maintain or will you build? Success requires you to steward your organisation to the future.

Rule 20

You will fail

London, England / Edinburgh, Scotland

It was a strange call in so many ways.

Here we were, unable to leave our homes again. Following the emergence of a new Covid variant the UK government had decided to impose another lockdown. This was the third time in less than a year that millions of us would watch the world through our windows as others were out there trying to save it. I was on a call with someone I was starting to know well. We had communicated several times either on the phone or online. We had never met in person.

At the onset of the first lockdown in March 2020, the government released a list of key occupations and workers who would be exempted from the most stringent restrictions. At the time Katherine and I were not surprised to see that leadership development experts didn't qualify as key workers.

When it comes to a pandemic everyone's focus is on the bottom of Maslow's hierarchy of needs. Management consultants, by and large, don't fulfil anyone's physiological needs. We were conscious that any support we might be able to give was of minimal value to those seeking, above all, safety. Yet, like so many, we too felt the urge to help and contribute.

We decided to do what we knew how to do, and suddenly had a lot of time to do – write a book. We hoped it would offer some ideas and guidance to those leaders who, as one of our clients had described it, were back to navigating by the stars. Our then publisher agreed to help and distribute it at cost so that it could reach the maximum number of people. In record time they mobilised and got the eBook 'Crisis Leadership' out. The call I was on came as a direct result of the book.

A civil servant, working in the UK National Health Service, had been a delegate at a conference I had spoken at several years before. After the conference he followed me on social media. When the book came out, he saw one of my posts about it and decided to read it. Having done so, he

DOI: 10.4324/9781032639390-24

reached out, first by email, with some thoughts and questions. We ended up having several calls.

Our conversations were mainly about how the book's contents could help him at different stages of the crisis the country was going through, and which he found himself at the forefront of solving. I am pretty sure, without any false modesty, that I didn't help a great deal in the face of so much turmoil. All I had to offer were a few moments of reflection, as I was sufficiently detached to see things differently and sufficiently in awe to offer him a brief respite from the constant pressure.

These were tough calls. I was trying to help in the moment but felt powerless overall. It's hard to be a spectator when you want to play your part. This one call wasn't just tough, though, it was strange. It stood out from the others which is why I haven't forgotten it.

At some stage during our conversation, my interlocutor said: 'We fail. People die.'

He didn't say it in the way a Hollywood hero would say it. He didn't mean 'and remember, if we fail, people die' in the way a superhero address-ing another would. It wasn't any kind of self-aggrandisement on his part to highlight the importance of his role. It wasn't said in a moment of despair either. He didn't say, 'and the worst of it is that we are failing people and when we fail, people die.' It was simply a factual description of what hap-pens in the world of medicine with some cases. If you fail to find a cure people die.

But this statement lit a bulb in my head that had never been lit before. It was strange that amongst all the trauma, hardship, and upheaval this civil servant was going through, all I thought about when he said 'We fail. People die' was that 'failure matters'. The man had just said people were dying and all I was thinking was 'failure matters'. I admit I felt, and still feel, rather awkward about my reaction so it warrants some explaining.

I am very familiar with the idea that it's ok to fail if we learn from it. This notion is encapsulated in the trendy saying 'fall often but fall for-ward' so loved by entrepreneurs and plastered on the walls of so many offices the world over. I am familiar with it but can't say I like it.

I know for a fact that if my doctor saves another patient because of the great lessons she learnt while messing up my diagnostic, I won't be filled with joy. Less dramatic but no less annoying, if I go to a restaurant and am served a terrible meal, it doesn't matter if the chef comes out of the kitchen to inform me that the apprentice who cooked it had learnt a great deal out of the experience. I won't be coming back to check on her progress.

By all means, make mistakes and learn from them, but make sure I am nowhere near that particular learning experience. Fail if you must, fall for-ward if you want, but please don't fall on me.

But my interlocutor hadn't said 'when we make mistakes or errors people die'. He had been clear. Faced with a new virus and emerging variants, doctors had reached the edge of their knowledge. Because they no longer knew what to do, people died. Because there was nothing left to try, people died. Because there was no known cure, people died.

In this case, he wasn't talking about mistakes or errors. He was talking about failure. With his simple statement he had opened my eyes to my own ambivalence about 'fall often but fall forward'. The mistake I was making, and which I know that too many leaders, too often, are making, was the inability to differentiate between mistakes and failures.

Our first rule was 'You can succeed'. I argued then that I could only be tentative with respect to the possibility of your success as I do not know you. I said that it would be dishonest to make a promise of success when I am not able to keep it. When it comes to failure, though, I can guarantee that you will fail.

There are times, arguably numerous times, where you will fall short of the goal you've set for yourself. This last rule is not about avoiding failure. That's impossible. It is about understanding the difference between failure and mistakes so that you can adopt the right mindset when either happens.

Mistakes are undesirable and should be avoidable. Failure isn't.

Imagine I want to run a marathon in under four hours. Instead, I abandon after 30 minutes. Have I failed? What about if I set out to sell 100 widgets and end up selling two? Have I failed? How about if I had run the marathon in 4 hours and 15 minutes and sold 90 widgets? Would I have failed?

If you have read this book so far in sequential order rather than jumping around, then you will know that the only possible answer to any of the above questions is 'it depends'. Don't get me wrong, I am not condoning underperformance or mediocrity. Instead, I am condemning flawed thinking and inertia. What will decide whether I have failed or not is whether I made a mistake or not.

What differentiates mistakes from failures is how you answer the question 'could I have done better?'.

If the answer to 'could I have done better?' is yes, you have not failed. Rather you have made one or more mistakes. The next question in the case of mistakes is 'why didn't you do better?'.

We must have made poor assumptions. The question we need to ask to move forward is 'What is it that I know now that I didn't know when you set the target'? Why did I think I could run so well or sell so much? It doesn't matter whether you missed the goal by a lot or by a bit. What matters is what we didn't know that we should have known when we set the target. A target is just the sum of assumptions. Only by identifying our shortfall in knowledge, skill, or will can we do better and not repeat the mistake.

In the case of my marathon example, maybe I thought I was in better shape than I am. Maybe I underestimated the effort required to run a marathon. Maybe I don't have the willpower it takes to push through the pain barrier. My mistake was due to a lack of understanding and/or consideration of readily available knowledge. I didn't consult enough, train enough, care enough, or know enough.

Mistakes are to be avoided and they can be avoided. In fact, in my experience, we are pretty good at doing so. We train people and design best in class processes. We are clear on the goal and objectives and set standards for how we want things done. We make other people stronger and more capable to engage them in the delivery of results. Many of the rules in our 'how' section help us to avoid mistakes.

Mistakes are an indication that we were not properly equipped when we set out on a course of action. Importantly, such mistakes would not have been made if we had fully used the knowledge available to us to better equip ourselves.

Sometimes, however, as was the case with my interlocutor on the call, the only possible answer to the question 'could I have done better?' is no.

This is when failure, rather than mistakes, becomes a key concept. A failure is what results when there is nothing I could have known that would have made the outcome better. It is not about having chosen the wrong course of action out of many possible options. A failure occurs when the only possible course of action yields the wrong result. When this happens, we must create new insights for future successes.

'We fail. People die' was not a statement of medical malpractice because of a mistake made. Instead, it was the acknowledgement of a failure that was being treated as call for further research and an intent for professional growth.

It is important to differentiate failures from mistakes because each requires a different kind of mindset and a different set of actions in order to be tackled. Failures require us to create new knowledge and new possibilities. Failures are not something that we can solve alone. They require bringing together all the resources at our disposal to search for answers and new possibilities.

Avoiding mistakes belongs in our 'how' section but embracing failure is all about the 'why'. Avoiding mistakes is something you can do by focusing on other people, or on you. Avoiding failures, however, requires everyone to focus on the issue. I'm not talking here about personal failings, but systemic failures. Arguably the reason we have leaders at all is to avoid failures, not to correct mistakes.

In fact, what my call highlighted to me – and it's why I wanted to close the book with this rule given the rule that opened it – is that success and failure are two sides of the same coin.

Let's get back to my exploits as a marathon-running salesperson. Having set out to meet my four-hour target, I manage – let's say – the marathon in 2 hours 45 minutes. Have I succeeded? What if I actually sell 200 widgets instead of the 100 I was aiming for? Have I succeeded? You know where I am going with this!

We may be quick to celebrate success, but we clearly messed up in setting our targets. We may be exceeding our targets, but we are still faced with significant variance between target and outcome. We didn't intend the outcome we obtained. The opposite of failure isn't success if the success is due to chance.

My interlocutor on the call could as easily have said 'We succeed. People live'. That would have been true and, indeed, much progress had been made in saving Covid patients by the time of the third UK lockdown. But if he had said this, the only way the achievement could be deemed a success would have been if doctors had known what it was they were doing that made people better. Luck is not the same as success in the same way that a mistake is not the same as failure.

At the end of the day, and at the end of this book, it is worth remembering that life, professional or otherwise, is just a collection of failures and successes. What determines whether or not a job is well done or a life is well lived is not the ratio between the two. It is whether successes or failures have led to greater wisdom. It is whether we have been intentional leaders who dug deep to understand success and avoid failure or just individuals who relied on luck and avoided mistakes. A job well done, or a life well lived, requires us to push forward the edge of the possible.

Maybe it is time we had new posters on our walls, displaying, in a bold, bright typeface, a new mantra. Succeed often but succeed forward!

From rule to lesson

Rule 20 – You will fail

When people talk about rules, they are either referring to instructions or to guidance. The former highlight to us what we are or aren't allowed to do. The latter outline principles we should follow to achieve a benefit of some kind. The 19 rules that precede this one fall into either of these categories.

There is, however, another definition of 'rule'. In this instance, a rule describes the way things happen in a given situation. We talk about the rules of English or those of science. Rule 20, our final rule, falls into this category. 'You will fail' is neither an instruction nor a principle: 'you will fail' is just a statement of fact.

The key to success is to understand that failure and mistakes are not the same. Mistakes can and should be avoided. They occur as a result of flawed execution. Minimising mistakes requires a relentless focus on meeting our 'how' rules. Failure, however, cannot be avoided. Failure occurs when there was no way of doing anything better in the current situation given the current available knowledge.

Failures are a 'why' issue as, while they cannot be avoided, success requires you to maintain a mindset of wanting to push forward the boundaries of the possible. It may be our final rule, but it is arguably our most important one. Without this kind of growth mindset, you will have neither the energy nor the resilience to succeed.

Conclusion – Now it's over to you

I take pride in tailoring all my speeches. Of course, the ideas will be similar, and some of the stories may be repeated. But the flow will always reflect the theme of the event, the make-up of the audience and the culture of the group I am addressing. I do this out of respect for the people who invite me to speak and the people who listen. I also do it to keep myself from getting into a routine where I take what I do for granted.

Even if I wanted to keep things the same, I realised early on that this would be impossible. I may the only one speaking but the people in the room are as responsible for what happens on stage as I am. Speakers feed off the energy of their audiences. I respond to the puzzled looks, the laughter, the heads that nod in approbation as well as those that nod off (it happens to the best of us).

But while I tailor all my speeches, I finish them all in exactly the same way, using the exact same words.

They are important words for me. They convey an idea I care about and want to spread. I never deviate. As I come to the end of this book however, I realise that I have never written these words down. I have never closed a book in the way I close a speech. Time for this to change. I apologise if you have heard me speak as you'll have heard it all before. I also apologise in advance if you ever hear me speak as you will have to hear it all again.

I always finish with a number. That number is 14600.

I don't know if you consider this a large or a small number. I guess it depends on what you associate with it. What if I tell you, though, that 14600 is, roughly, the number of days you have left to live? Before you do your own sums and decide that I am out by several days (either way) know that I am basing the number of the average global lifespan of about 73.16 years and the average age of those in an audience sitting somewhere around 33.

I am not an actuary. Sometimes, in the case of my speeches, and maybe, in the case of this book, someone will argue about the exact number.

DOI: 10.4324/9781032639390-25

Despite the purist's reservations about its validity, I am sure all can agree that it feels small, especially if we think about how many of these days we live being healthy and able.

I often think about a speaker from the Mayo clinic I had the privilege of sharing a stage with who reminded us of our propensity to think of our increasing lifespan as being made up of good days rather than the reality that it was 'our frailty rather than our youth medicine was lengthening'.

I do not finish speeches by reminding audiences of their mortality out of some twisted humour. I do it to remind them of the importance of their lives.

In 2003 I conducted a survey involving mainly US residents. The aim was to gather information rather than conduct research. I wanted to understand what people regret. I wanted to ask, 'what would you do differently if you could start your life again?' I ended up collecting data from over a thousand people, all over the age of 65. Responses ranged in content, length, and depth, but three clear themes quickly became apparent. Over 75% of respondents gave me the same three answers.

- I would take time to stop and ask the big questions.
- I would be more courageous and take more risks in work and love.
- I would try to live with purpose, make a difference.

My penultimate slide is always the same (my last slide has just my email on it). It shows the number 14599 over a rotating earth. My question is always 'why wait?'. Why wait until we are over 65, starting to regret the things we now know we will regret, to do something about them?

So let me ask the same question as we come to the end of this book. Why wait?

Why wait to take the time to stop and ask the big questions?

We are all busy people with complicated lives. We all have things that need to be done and obligations that need to be met. We have commitments we can't get out of and problems we struggle to resolve. We spend time and energy solving issues so that tomorrow is better, even though we will have less time and energy to enjoy it.

Stopping to take stock matters as it offers perspective and perspective is key to making the right choices. Yet, we are afraid to stop. But stopping doesn't have to be a long pause. Stopping can be a few minutes in the day just to ask ourselves 'am I doing the right thing? am I focusing on what matters?'. Stopping helps us spot what matters.

Asking the big questions makes us do something about what matters. Anyone who has worked anywhere will know that any group of people has a life and a language of its own. There is a beat to an organisation. It has a cadence. It has a pace. It doesn't take long for anyone to march to that beat. Only when we stop can we question the beat.

In A. A. Milne's Winnie-the-Pooh we are introduced to the iconic bear when Christopher Robin, half awake, comes down the stairs in his pyjamas, dragging it along by the ear, with its head bouncing on each stair tread. We are told that Winnie is thinking, 'It is, as far as he knows, the only way of coming downstairs, but sometimes he feels that there really is another way, if only he could stop bumping for a moment and think of it.' We are all Winnies.

We have all had moments where we thought, 'If only my head could stop hurting for a second, I am sure I could find a better way. If only I had more time I could come up with a better solution. If only I'd had the resources, it would have been different. If only I didn't have to sort "A" out, I could have taken care of "B".' 'If only' is the only possible outcome if we do not stop to ask the big questions.

I have outlined the rules and, hopefully, made them practical enough for you to decide on some of the actions you would like to take, but I can't take them for you. If you want to succeed you will have to stop, ask yourself the big questions, reflect, decide, and act. In that order! You can't do it in any other order. Action without question and intent is just activity.

When it comes to taking the time to stop, and asking the big questions, it's over to you.

Why wait to be more courageous and take more risks in work and love?

If there is one lesson coming out of every rule in this book, it is that success in leading is about courage and risks. Luck doesn't help unless the opportunities it offers are seized. This takes courage and is risky. Skills don't help unless they are applied. This takes courage and is risky. To lead is to stand out, and standing out takes courage and is risky. Courage is not foolhardiness. It is not about taking unnecessary risks. Courage is about being able to do something that frightens us, like going with what luck offers, displaying our skills, or standing out.

There is, however, another lesson implied in all the stories I have told. It is a lesson about the nature of risk. Every action, decision, and choice made by the people I introduced you to was only risky before it was taken. All of them were proven to be far less risky in hindsight. This is why courage and risk go together. It is only by having the courage to take them that you can see the true nature of the risks you take.

But the people in the above survey didn't just talk about work, they talked also about love. As I mentioned in Rule 3, leading is an exchange of energy. It is about you injecting your energy into the system. Like a battery that empties itself, our energy depletes as the day goes by. Where do we refuel? For many, our energy comes from our loved ones. We refuel at home and empty at work. Yet, unless we bring energy back from our work how will those at home feel? We can't just take without giving back.

It takes courage to talk about love and it seems risky to see our lives at work and at home as interconnected. We prefer to talk about work-life balance as if the two could exist separately from each other. The truth is work and life can't even coexist, they are one and the same. It is your life. To succeed in both work and love is about taking the risk to want to do both well. Without love to fuel you, you will not successfully lead at work. It is only by taking the risk to love who you are, who you are with, and what you do that you will have the courage to lead.

When it comes to being more courageous, and taking more risks in work and love, it's over to you.

Why wait to try to live with purpose, make a difference?

I have always been ambivalent about the idea of living with purpose. I find the idea of a life well lived, or at least one lived with intent, appealing. Yet I find that, in practice, life is a collection of successive days spent trying to do my best, be mindful, helpful, and kind, but with no overarching plan towards some great achievement.

Living with purpose seems easier for anyone with a vocation. If you have a calling, pursuing your passion makes sense. If you don't, as I believe is the case for most of the people I meet, the search for purpose can prove elusive. Does this mean we are bound to experience this last of the three regrets, of not living a life of enough purpose, of not making enough difference?

Over the years, I have come to realise that purpose is not some grand design. It is not about 'saving the world' or working towards world peace. Lofty goals and idealistic aims are not unnecessary, nor are they the domain of the romantic. To succeed, especially given that leadership is all about our impact on others, we must believe in something greater than ourselves. This is why the 'making a difference' part of the regret is important.

We do not have to feel impotent in the face of global, towering challenges. But we need to remember one thing. Thinking about 'the big stuff' is only of value if you are prepared to commit to act on 'the small stuff'. We all have an ability to influence our surroundings. Whether to a small or a large extent, we can be agents of local change even if not all of us will get to be masters of global outcomes.

This is our power. We can choose to make other people stronger and more capable. We can choose to impact the world around us. Success does not lie in our achievements but in our endeavours. Our purpose is to try to make a difference. As one CEO I worked with told me, '80% of the time you'll, more or less, get it right. The hard part is to learn to forgive yourself for the other 20%.'

Your purpose is not some external, grand, moral goal that someone else can dictate for you. It is the internal struggle to understand what makes you distinctive and the willingness to use this to make a difference to others.

When it comes to living with purpose, making a difference, it's over to you.

Books are written to inform but they also deceive. This is the most personal book I have written. I have introduced you to some of the people I have met and some of the lessons I have learnt from them. All these reflections are true. The deception lies in the fact that it makes my life seem orderly, planned, and informed.

Just as the fireside chat that I mentioned in my introduction to Part 1 did, this book makes it sound as though I have been going around spending my life researching, recording, and reflecting. This is simply not true.

Life has been incredibly kind to me. I am not particularly insightful or clever. I have benefited from the accident of birth and the hazards of life others have not been so lucky to receive. I recognise that I am both privileged and fortunate, but I also know that I am far from perfect. Most of these lessons I learnt too late. Some rules became obvious only after repeated mistakes. I hope that by laying them out for you in the way I have it will make it simpler for you to adopt them. And I wish you the very best in your endeavours.

* * *

'As for the future, your task is not to foresee it, but to enable it.'[1]

I started my second book, *Leadershift*, with this quote from the French writer and adventurer Antoine de Saint-Exupéry, and it seems appropriate to use it again to close this book, given that my focus here is on taking the first step. There is no right or wrong future. There is just whatever happens next.

Note

1   Translated by the author. 'L'avenir, tu n'as point à le prévoir mais à le permettre.' Antoine de Saint-Exupéry, *Citadelle* (la Pleiade, Œuvres complètes, tome II, Editions Gallimard 1999), chapter 56, p. 503.

Index